MAKE A WAY FINANCIAL LIBRARY

START A HOME BUSINESS IN 30 DAYS

MAKE A WAY® MINISTRIES INC

Start a Home Business in 30 Days

Copyright © October 2017 by Dr. William Miller

MAKE A WAY® PUBLISHING
Miami, Florida

MAKE A WAY® MINISTRIES is a nonprofit Christian Ministry

Operating Office Mailing Address:	Corporate Office:
P.O. Box 1164	12030 SW 129 Court
Granbury, Texas 76048	Suite 104
	Miami, Florida 33186

1-800-357-4223

www.makeaway.net
www.creditcounseling.net

All Rights Reserved:

This publication has been prepared in the United States of America. All rights are reserved under International Copyright Law. No part of this publication may be reproduced or transmitted in any form or by any means, electronic or mechanical, including photocopying, recording, or by any information storage and retrieval system, without the written permission of the publisher. Permission will not be withheld if the objective of the request is to disseminate information at no cost to the recipient. Such disseminations must convey the entire publication contained herein including this statement.

PRINTED IN THE UNITED STATES OF AMERICA
All rights reserved under international copyright laws

ISBN-10: 1979170444
ISBN-13: 978-1979170444

Introduction

I'm of the opinion that every family in America should consider starting their own home-based business. The main reason is that the tax system in this country is set up to encourage the formation of small private business but many people don't ever take advantage of it. And, any future tax system that comes along is going to be just as pro-small business as the present system, if not more so because the financial strength of this country is closely tied to our small business sector.

Even if you work for an employer full time, there's an important tax advantage available for people who just set up a home-based business that they then pursue in their spare time. If you don't have one, you are paying the U.S. government what is in effect a "donation" because you're GIVING them taxes they have made arrangements for you to not pay. Why take money away from your family and give it to the government when you don't have to? The fact is, they would prefer that you start a business!

In case you didn't know, the formation of home-based businesses is the fastest growing commercial sector in the country. Something else you may not know is that small businesses in this country account for almost half of our business activity and 70 percent of them started in somebody's home. Yes, many huge companies started in somebody's home and that could happen to you too.

But, you have to start something. You have to take a first step if you want to get somewhere. This book can be a big help for getting started on the road to success. Your future is waiting and only you can make it happen!

Dedication

This book is dedicated to future entrepreneurs who will boldly step out to start their home businesses but have the wisdom to pursue knowledge and prepare themselves adequately for future success.

Content

Introduction	3
Dedication	4
1. The Significance of Home Based Business	7
2. Deciding to Make a Change	13
3. The Importance of the Free Enterprise System	19
4. Why You Should Start a Home Based Business	29
5. Steps for Starting a Home Based Business	39
6. Basics for Writing a Business Plan	53
7. Types of Organizations	59
8. How to Build Startup Credit	69
9. Other Essential Financial Issues	77
10. How to Minimize Personal Indebtedness	87
11. Setting Aside Cash Reserves	105
12. Importance of Giving Your Business to God	115
13. Some Final Thoughts	119
Appendix One: How to Apply for an SBA Loan	124
Appendix Two: Financial Statements for Beginners	137
Appendix Three: Eight Secrets of Financial Success	149
About the Author	167

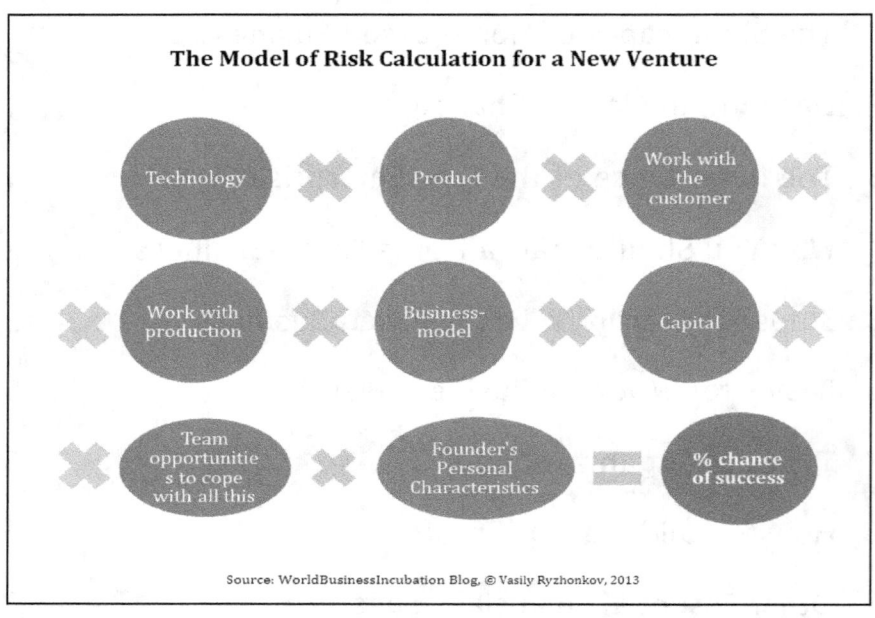

1. The Significance of Home Based Business

The fastest growing business sector in America is the business that's conducted from homes by full and part time entrepreneurs. This is a notable fact that people easily overlook because large business draws most of our attention. Indeed, home businesses account for almost half a trillion dollars per year in sales volume through more than 38 million home-based companies. The top 20 percent of them enjoy annual incomes in the range of $100,000 to $500,000.[1]

How would you like to make a half million dollars per year working a lot of the time in your PJ's? And, you would be working on things that you actually like to do. And, you would be making your own decisions. And, you wouldn't have a boss more interested in his/her career than yours. And, you could take a vacation with your family any time you wanted to for as long as you could afford to. Are you open to any of that?

Millions of people are trying it out by starting a home-based business while they continue working full time for an employer. That's a good strategy because it protects the family's income until the home-based side-business you're operating in your spare time is able to provide for ALL of the family's financial needs. History shows that

---

[1] https://www.incfile.com/blog/post/shocking-us-home-based-business-statistics/

strategy works because 70 percent of all companies started off as a home-based business.[2] They started out in somebody's home, they got bigger and sold more over a period of time, the founders quit their day jobs and went full time with the home business and eventually many of them got too big for the home and had to move into an office somewhere close to the new bigger and more luxurious home they are now buying. Maybe they can't wear their PJ's to work anymore but their income on average is probably exceeding $250,000 per year and that's a worthwhile tradeoff for your silk PJ's.

The Odds of Success

The strategy of a having a home-based startup phase had a VERY significant influence on the typical rise to the top I'm describing in the previous paragraph. And here's how that worked. Studies show that more than 70 percent of all small businesses FAIL during their first five years of life. Most of that is in the first two years. But if they started out as home-based businesses, the odds change dramatically because coincidentally 70 percent of all home-based businesses SUCCEED. In sum, if folks will just slow down a little and go through a home-based startup stage, the entrepreneur goes from a 25-30 percent chance of success to a 70 percent probability of success. Now, that's worth considering![3]

---

[2] https://smallbiztrends.com/2013/07/home-based-businesses-startup.html
[3] https://www.incfile.com/blog/post/shocking-us-home-based-business-statistics/

So, why do you suppose such a high percentage of small businesses fail? Indeed, 70 percent is HIGH! The main reason is that too many hopeful entrepreneurs don't know enough about financial management. They needed knowledge and lost their money because they jumped out in an area they didn't have experience in. Managing the finances of your own business is a "night and day" difference from managing the secure salary or commission you receive from your employer. You need to know something about business finances or you are LIKELY to fail. Indeed, three-fourths of them DO fail. That is the simple reality!

Since they don't know enough about finances, they use their startup capital inefficiently. They use it up too fast and wind up as a negative statistic: their businesses failed because they were under-capitalized. But the truth is, they didn't know enough about business finances and used their limited startup capital inefficiently. You need capital to run a business and if it gets used up, the business fails.

Also, since they didn't know enough about business finances, they overestimated the amount of business income that would be available to take home to their families. So, some of their startup capital had to be withdrawn to make ends meet at home which contributed to the failure of the business.

The story could have been entirely different if they had taken their new business ideas through a home-business phase while they continued working for their employer(s). The hands-on experience of the home-based business would have provided a practical way to learn the ins-and-outs of the VERY complex financial industry and thus changed the overwhelming odds for failure into an overwhelming probability of success.

The Clincher

There is yet another step you could take to make your success virtually assured: you can learn some basics about the finances associated with running a business and according to market studies the odds for success increase to 93+ percent.[4] In fact, that success rate is for all small business added together. If you go through the step of a part time home-based startup phase at the beginning of your company and add in a basic understanding of business finances as well, the odds are more like a 98 percent probability that you will succeed at whatever you try.

Where are you going to learn what you need to know about business finances? Part of it will come from operating your own part time home-based business for a while. Also, reading this book will give you a lot of what your need to start with so read and study it carefully. We also have a deeper book on business finance you could purchase called: *Employee to Employer in 90 Days*. Look for it on Amazon.com at the following Link:

---

[4] *"Starting and Running a Profitable Small Business,"* Texas Wesleyan University

https://www.amazon.com/Employee-Employer-Days-BillMiller/dp/1518622410/ref=sr_1_8?ie=UTF8&qid=1509049925&sr=8-8&keywords=Dr.+Bill+Miller

Friend, this is only possible in America. Take advantage of it and learn why this is the most economically successful country in the history of the world.

2. Deciding to Make a Change

For a couple of years now, I've been telling folks in any of our workshops that I think <u>every family in America</u> should own a home-based business. Most new ventures should start out as home-based businesses where they will learn the basics before going out to find office space and try to become big operations. That makes it important to consider the house you own as a business investment and as the place from where you will soon be operating a successful business. You need to SEE your business operating in your house. Find a way to make it work. If you are considering a new hours, SEE your business operating in it BEFORE you buy. Not all houses are going to be an optimal location for a going business even on a part time basis but do the best you can.

Studies show that 70 percent of all Americans want to be in business for themselves.[5] It seems like every statistic in the Small Business sector turns out to be 70 percent but that's what it is. The 70 percent who would like to own their own business compares to the 30 or so percent that actually own one. Why is there such a disparity between wishing and doing? Not even half of the people who are dreaming about owning their own business are actually doing it.

---

[5] https://www.incfile.com/blog/post/shocking-us-home-based-business-statistics/

The truth is, everybody has to take the first step to start a process of change and people have a lot of trouble taking that first step. Moreover, they become secure in the scenario of working for others and have trouble busting out of the cocoon of being somebody's employee. Every business venture involves risk and leaving the security of being an employee is perceived as risky by most people. They don't realize that with a good idea and some basic preparation, the risk can be reduced to the point that it makes little sense to not try to enter the ranks of the self-employed.

There are a number of reasons for wanting to be self-employed and we'll look at those in a later chapter. But first you have to be willing to take the first step and make a change in your way of THINKING. The Bible says that as a person thinks in his/her heart, so is he/she.[6] Each of us are today the result of how we've been thinking. Do we put limits on ourselves? Are we afraid of change? Do we fear trying something new? What is holding back millions of Americans who say they want to be in business for themselves from actually doing it?

Friend, there are 85 million single-family homes in America that are NOT hosting a family business. Out of that group there are about 50 million that say they WANT to own a business and the remaining folks aren't interested and prefer to continue doing whatever it is they're already doing. We need to look at a few very real

---
[6] Proverbs 23:7

reasons people are opting out of such a great and virtually irresistible opportunity.

Here are some of the main reasons folks are holding back but certainly not all of them:

1. They don't believe they can succeed.
2. They are not willing to give up their security.
3. They don't know what to do to start one.
4. It has never happened in their families before.
5. Or, it did happen in their family one time and failed.
6. They are conditioned to being poor and limited.
7. They want to start something but they procrastinate.
8. They believe it is too risky.
9. They are overwhelmed by their lack of knowledge.

Since you are reading this book, I'm going to assume that you are part of the 85 million on the outside looking in but that you're considering a jump to the ranks of the self-employed. The message I have for you is that I can show you how to set up a home-based business that is almost guaranteed to succeed with a reasonable chance for the future to grow out of your house and into an office where you can develop a successful business that could last for generations. Part of that depends on your age, the younger the better, and another part is related to your individual ability to absorb new information and put it into practice.

It all starts with a first step and here's why I tell our workshops that every home in America should own a home-based business: it an unbelievably easy path to additional income. All you have to do is register a company name in the official record of your state, open a company bank account and start up an office in your home. By doing just that most people will then be eligible for tax deductions that have been created by our federal government precisely to encourage the growth and prosperity of American small business. That's the way our country works. Our government has created all kinds of ways to reduce income taxes and a relative few are taking advantage of it.

In sum, the biggest thing holding people back from business and financial success is their thinking. They THINK it's too risky. They THINK they can't succeed. Or, they THINK they should stay with the security.

A number of years ago I left college and went to work for one of the largest corporations in the world. My goal was to work for that company for five years and then return to my home town and go into private business with my family. When the five years finished way quicker than I had expected, I decided to go another five years because I was enjoying the security of a bi-weekly or monthly paycheck and I had access to a bunch of benefits that represented additional income. Before I knew what had happened I was approaching my 20th anniversary in that company and I hated it. Every day I hated the corporate environment, I hated all the office politics and I hated every moment of not being in business for myself. I was one of the 70 percent of American business people who long to be in business for themselves but have trouble pulling the trigger on that first step. I wanted to leave that company but I kept on procrastinating.

Fortunately, that first step was taken for me because that company decided I didn't fit into their future operating plans and I was offered early retirement. I took it, left the company in my rear view mirror and went on down a new road to self-employment. I couldn't seem to come up with the courage to pull the trigger myself so the company I'd worked for 20 years pulled it for me. It was like being set free with new air to breathe!

I give you this testimony to encourage you to get your thinking right. I can show you how to succeed in a small business startup as almost a sure things. Of course, there are situations that come along in this world that we can't control, but barring some catastrophe, you CAN do this. And even if you DO fail, you can come back and start something else. Walt Disney failed 7 times before he finally hit on the right thing. As an inventor, Thomas Edison made 1,000 unsuccessful attempts at inventing the light bulb. Success is NEVER guaranteed but there are ways to maximize your odds of winning and we have most of them covered in this book!

Think about your life and what you want to do with it Take control of it instead of just letting it happen. And then make something notable out of it, not for yourself but to glorify God and help Him build His Kingdom.

> THE RIGHT TO
> PROFIT FREELY
> AND BELIEF IN GOD
> ARE THE ESSENTIAL
> BASES OF FREE ENTERPRISE

2. The Importance of the Free Enterprise System

Starting a small business will put you smack in the middle of America's free enterprise system. It just happens to be THE economic system that has produced the highest standard of living in the history of the world and you are thinking about how to become a bigger part of it so you can receive more from it like so many millions of people have before you. Some have succeeded and some have failed, but as mentioned in the previous chapter, one of the great things about our system is that if you fail, you can get up and try again. And you can keep trying until you finally experience the fulfillment of all your personal dreams and aspirations.

Most people in the world don't have this opportunity because they aren't FREE on a political level. Instead of governing themselves, they have rulers who have taken away their FREEDOM and imposed controls over the details of whatever economic system they have in place. By instituting controls though, the motivation for personal achievement is stifled and people stop trying to succeed financially when the profit incentive has been removed or become so controlled and regulated that only a few can achieve success.

We live in a time when everything is criticized by somebody. The Free Enterprise System is not exempted from the criticism but most of the people doing the criticizing have no clue what they're talking about. They don't actually DO much of anything except take what they can get from other people while living their lives for the most part being uninformed and lacking in wisdom. Instead of doing something constructive to lift themselves out of their failures, they stand by blaming others and criticizing everything they can think of including the best economic system in world history that they've decided not to be a part of. Many of them want to be Socialists and have the government run everything and the reason is that they're too lazy to perform some basic research on the Internet to find out about all the failure Socialism has produced for ALL the others who've tried it throughout history. Or, they're not lazy at all and want to use Socialism as the means for taking away the wealth of others for their own gain.

If this sounds a bit harsh, it's here precisely written for that purpose. As soon as you start your own home-based business, you join a unique community that produces most of the wealth for our country. At the same time you will be putting yourself in the line of fire that comes from all the blamers, doubters, malcontents, defeatists, criticizers and takers the world has to offer. You need to learn about this great system we have and be prepared to defend it against all the people who want to ruin it with their regulations and excessive taxation that they need for funding all their government give-away programs and to redistribute the country's wealth from those who have created it to those who are either unable or unwilling to create or work for their own wealth. There is a big difference between folks who are unable to create their own wealth and those who are busy trying to confiscate somebody else's wealth. Be ready to help those who need help and resist those who are TAKERS.

The Common Criticisms

There are a few things that Free Enterprise is always criticized for that we have just enough limited space to cover in this particular publication:

1. The first criticism is that the Free Enterprise System creates distance between the rich and poor. That is only true if the poor don't try to lift themselves out of their poverty by taking advantage of what the system can provide. If they go to the government for their provision instead of working through the Free Enterprise System for its potential, they will surely stay in their poverty. We need for more and more people to take advantage of starting their own small businesses instead of becoming dependent on the government dole that only produces poor people.

2. Another area of criticism is the fact that there is risk involved in the pursuit of free enterprise. But risk is directly related to FREE markets. And, profit potential is directly related to the amount of risk: the more risk in a venture, the greater the profit potential. Yes, there is always the risk of failure, but there is also as a

direct result the potential for greater economic success. Profit is a reward to the risk-taker.

3. Another criticism is that there are economic cycles involved. There are times of plenty but there are also down turns, recessions and occasionally a depression. A FREE economic system will always move in cycles but a great deal of the downward pressure on growth cycles and the negative pressure in the world's economies is caused by government interference and over-regulation that produce uncertainty. The greatest cause of economic failure is UNCERTAINTY.

4. A fourth criticism is that business people only respond to profit which makes them greedy people. The fact is a FREE economy produces profits and the greater the profits are, the more that can be made available for charitable giving. The greatest source of giving in the country is the pool of capitalistic profit produced by successful privately owned businesses.

5. People who are owners of business are immoral. The truth is the opposite especially when the system is based on biblical principles of life and enterprise. Jesus talked extensively about money and property and contrary to popular belief, He wasn't telling everyone they should be poor.

The bottom line for this chapter is that we should be eager to join the ranks of small business people but quick to defend our system of Free Enterprise when it comes under attack, which is pretty much constantly. It would help to study about it so you can know what you've become a part of and why you want to stay there in the face of all the criticism you'll be hearing. Following is some basic information that you can refer to in the future from *The Social Studies Help Center.*[7]

Basic Principles of Free Enterprise

Now, the U.S. economic system of free enterprise operates according to five main principles:

1. Freedom to Choose Our Own Business

In this country, the decision to go into a particular business is yours alone to make. You will decide what prices to charge and what your working hours are. Certain laws prohibit you from cheating or damaging your customers or other people. But in theory you will be left alone to run your business as you want.

2. Right to Own Private Property

Private property can be a parcel of land, a home, or a car or any other asset that is owned by an individual, a family or group. It differs from public property like a city hall, a park, or a highway which provide a government service for all citizens. In the U.S. economic system, the right of people to buy and sell private property is guaranteed by law. But generally people do not have the right to use

---

[7] http://www.socialstudieshelp.com/eco_Free_enterprise.htm

their private property to interfere with the property rights of others or to harm them in some way. There are of course exceptions in applying this basic principle according to local practice and legislation consistent with federal constitutional law.

3. Profit Motive

The main reason for starting a small business is to make money. You make profit by taking in more money than you spend. The amount of money left over after subtracting your business expenses from your business income is called your profit. In the free enterprise system, business firms try hard to keep costs down and increase their sales revenue. The better they succeed at this, the higher their profits will be. Economists describe the efforts by business firms to earn the greatest profits as the "profit motive" and you do NOT have to apologize if you're motivated to make profit. Since it is private, what you do with your profit is your private concern even though takers will be trying constantly to tell you what you should do with your personal profit. The fact is the government encourages small business formation so that there will be ongoing future sources of tax revenue and to pay for their grandiose programs.

4. Competition

Just as you are free to start your own small business, so is everybody else. The rivalry among sellers in the same field to attract consumer dollars is called competition. If your business is profitable, it is likely others will enter the same type of small business hoping to be as successful as you. They will be competing with you for the same customers. To win a share of the particular market segment you are operating in, other sellers may try to offer more and better services or at lower prices. Because of the pressure of competition, business firms must constantly try to provide the best services and create the best products at the lowest possible prices.

5. Sovereignty of the Customer

In the end, it is the customers, the consumers who determine whether any business succeeds or fails. In the U.S. free enterprise economy, consumers are said to have sovereignty which is the power or freedom to have final say. Consumers are free to spend their money for your products or somebody else's products. If they prefer somebody else over you, then your company may lose money, go out of business or decide to market some different product or service. And so, how consumers choose to spend their available dollars causes business firms of all kinds to produce certain goods and services and not others.

Adopting a Code of Conduct

Many entrepreneurs assume that the morals of private enterprise will be automatically adjusted by forces in the marketplace. In other words consumers will eventually tend to gravitate away from immoral small businesses that profit by cheating consumers over to businesses that follow an ill-defined but acceptable Code of Conduct. But I differ with that view because I believe that the best system for anything in life will ALWAYS be based on a biblically-based model that depends on honesty and deference to others. Even though this book isn't intended as a Christian Bible study, I would be remiss if I didn't tell you that the system that will produce the greatest profitability for you long term is the FREE system of private capitalism that has incorporated a Christian, bible-based view of business.

The purpose of this book is to help you start and operate a small business successfully. Small business provides a wonderful opportunity for financial and personal success if you start off right, if you are fair to others and if you understand how the marketplace works based on the principles outlined in this publication. Appreciating the value of the free enterprise system and defending it in the face of its enemies is an essential component. It isn't taught in schools and most of the current day culture can scarcely describe it for you. But if you understand it and how blessed you are to have access to it, your probability of success just went up another notch. No other kind of economic system will let you do what we're considering together in this book. So, make the most of it and prepare for success!

ONE OF THE BEST REASONS I CAN THINK OF
TO BE A SMALL BUSINESS OWNER

4. Why You Should Start a Home Based Business

As we've already seen in previous chapters, there are some really good reasons to start one's own business. For one thing, those that *do* ultimately succeed usually wind up being a lot more financially well off than their counterparts who work for someone else. Statistics show that the income levels of successful entrepreneurs are at least 50% higher on average than comparable folks who're working for others and 50% higher than the salary they had with the company they worked for before they started their own businesses.

The successful ones eventually get to the place where they can take a few days off once in a while. And, there's a great deal of satisfaction derived from watching one's "baby" grow up to become a viable and successful adult. If you follow our recommendations, you will start with your humble little part time business at home and over time you will nurture it into a big success outside the home with employees and branch offices and whatever other prosperity the Lord brings into your life.

There's also the fact that once you get rolling along in your own company once it can support you financially, you won't have to worry about being down-sized and laid off suddenly without income. In general, the highs of entrepreneurship are higher than the highs of working for somebody else. But occasionally the lows can be lower. When things are going good, the entrepreneur is euphoric; in times of crisis there's desperation and concern and worry and indecisiveness and lack of sleep. The biggest challenge is to get the business to a point where you can get rid of those lows!

The truth is, owning your own small business can and should be an exciting, challenging and rewarding experience, and there are at least seven important reasons for you to consider starting one as soon as you can:

1. The pursuit of <u>Independence</u> is the first reason and it includes freedom from having your future in someone else's hands, freedom from endless meetings where little is ever accomplished, freedom from dealing with the never-ending emergencies of the bosses instead of following your own priorities, freedom from office politics and backbiting and interacting with all those difficult people every day and freedom from having to make money for somebody else's pocket instead of yours. You'll also like the freedom of setting your own schedule so you can work the hours you want to.

   But most of all, you'll no longer be DEPENDENT upon others and under their control in the pursuit of your personal goals and objectives. You'll be free to allow God to lead you to your destiny without interference from a less interested employer who requires you to work toward their company's goals and objectives sometimes in ways that violate your sense of values and direction.

2. The second reason for starting a small business is to enjoy the <u>challenge</u> of having something fun to do where you can be creative and receive the benefits of your creativity. Also, other people will no longer be able to take credit for your ideas.

3. The third reason to start small business is to have a better testimony. For some reason, people who are self-employed are looked up to in our society, even if your business is a home-based business. It's like a status symbol. Even if you're struggling in your self-employment, you'll be looked up to and admired for trying to make something happen on your own especially if it's known that God is your CEO. The truth is, the people who're working for others that you come in contact with will be ENVIOUS of what you're trying to accomplish. They see you and wish they had the boldness and the courage to try it themselves.

4. The fourth reason is that there are <u>NO external restrictions or requirements</u> for the owner of a small business to have to deal with as there often are working for others. External restrictions and requirements include the amount of education you have, what gender you are, your age or race or background, etc. Any of these things can hold people back in their careers and RESTRICT their advancement even when their job performance is excellent.

5. Another really good reason is that owning a small business can help you <u>build an estate</u> for your family

to a much higher level than would be typical working for somebody else. You will be building something substantial for the generations of your progeny to own and benefit from in the future

6. Owning your own business may also allow you to spend more time with your spouse and children, particularly if you provide them with employment. If you decide to run a home-based small business, you will also be freeing up much of your time and expense that were used in commuting to an employer's office.

7. Finally, every family should consider starting a small business as a way of <u>reducing the amount of federal tax</u> you pay so you can redirect those funds to expansion of your retirement savings or back into the operation of your home-based business. This is a really important topic that should be emphasized: virtually ALL families in America could and *should* OWN A SMALL BUSINESS FOR THE PURPOSE OF TAX OPTIMIZATION. The U.S. Congress and the U.S. Internal Revenue Service have structured the tax code to favor and encourage the formation of small businesses. So why would we not organize ourselves to get the maximum benefit out of the economic system that's been set up? Why would we insist on paying more taxes than we legally have to by ignoring a principal means that's been created precisely for the purpose of encouraging American entrepreneurs to start new businesses? And, it's better for the country!

ILLUSTRATION: EFFECT OF SMALL BUSINESS OWNERSHIP ON PERSONAL INCOME TAX

The following chart illustrates in a simple way why we recommend that EVERY family in America consider starting a small business. From the very beginning, whether your business makes a profit or not, you are eligible for business tax deductions that will generate a positive cash flow for your family. All you have to do is form the company and register it with the state. Take a look at this basic comparison and study it carefully:

	Employee Only	Small Business Owner (DBA)
Revenue:		
Salary from W-2 Employer	$30,000	30,000
Income from Own Business	- 0 -	- 0 -
(Small Business assumed to break even)		
Business Deductions:		
Business Trips (vacation)	- 0 -	2,000
Children on Payroll	- 0 -	4,000
Automobile	- 0 -	4,000
Office in Home	- 0 -	3,000
Entertainment (one-half)	- 0 -	2,000
Purchase of Equipment	- 0 -	5,000
Miscellaneous	- 0 -	2,000
Adjusted Gross Income:	$30,000	8,000
Federal Taxes:		
Income Taxes	2,800	- 0 -
Social Security	2,250	1,200
Total Taxes Paid	5,050	1,200

The illustration on the previous page shows that the tax savings from operating a small business out of this family's home while continuing to work for a W-2 employer was $3,850 via the tax reduction from taking advantage of LEGAL small business deductions to reduce the amount of income that is subject to taxation.[8]

According to IRS Tax Regulations the small business owner is allowed to take business deductions when the following criteria are met:

>The deductions are legal
>The deductions are ordinary for the industry
>The deductions are reasonable
>The deductions are for necessary expenses

Just so you know, there are presently more than 120 legal tax deductions for small businesses embedded somewhere in the 93 thousand pages of the IRS Tax Code. Indeed, the foregoing example only scratches the surface of what small business people can learn about tax optimization. And, if someday the government were to reform the IRS Tax Code, it is almost certain they would focus on the reduction of small business tax rates and leave in place most or all of the current deductions.

In sum, it will be poor stewardship of God's money to not start a small business unless of course He's telling you not to for other reasons. Pray about it, take it to the Lord and if He releases you into small business ownership, you

---

[8] *"Starting and Running a Profitable Small Business,"* Texas Wesleyan University

could join the millions of people who're taking this route to make more funds available through the reduction of their taxes.

Special Thoughts for Christian Entrepreneurs

From a Christian perspective, it is our hope that more Believers will aspire to small business ownership because when you're working for someone else, you become dependent on your employer instead of on God. As long as you're employed, your salary payments arrive every week or two automatically and you enjoy certain benefits that are at least partially paid for by your employer. You become involved in a career and the health of your career instead of the health of your spirit. If you're asked to transfer to a new location and you turn it down, your career will suffer. So you will tend to accept job transfers without regarding the possibility that God might want you to stay where you are. You accept job transfers to receive a salary increase without considering that God is your real Provider. It's often difficult for Believers to work for someone else and remain pure in their faith.

By being in business for yourself, you can also work on what God tells you is best for the Kingdom of God and on commercial activities that are consistent with your callings and abilities. You won't be a square peg in a round hole unless you get there by a wrong decision, but if that happens you can just go find a square hole.

If you're reading this book and you KNOW that your destiny is to be self-employed, go on and start preparing yourself for it. Make it your personal goal that you're constantly working toward. Eventually you WILL succeed and then you'll be really glad you took a chance. I believe most people are called to own small business. God has given you wisdom and witty inventions for the purpose of establishing His kingdom. The time will come, perhaps it's now, to step out in faith and pursue your destiny. All you have to do is start a home-based business, start enjoying the increased cash from tax optimization and you're on your way!

5. Steps for Starting a Home-Based Business

As already discussed, the most difficult thing about starting a small business is taking the first step. Even with me assuring you that you can start and operate one out of your own home with greater than a ninety percent chance of success if you do what we advise, it's still difficult to actually implement something. And that's especially true when you'll be taking action that could profoundly change your life from the path you're presently on.

Anybody can have ideas. People talk among themselves all the time sharing their ideas, discussing their creativity and things they would like to do...someday. But most of that "creative" thinking never goes anywhere. There has to be implementation before anything of value can be produced. You MUST make an irrevocable decision that you're going to take action. You make a decision that you want to change your life and be in business for yourself as a lifetime goal. Most people start home-based businesses with the goal of earning additional income in the short term. I'm advising you to think bigger and go for a longer term goal of becoming a successful business entrepreneur that you're going to get to step-by-step. By setting higher goals for yourself, you are more likely to get beyond the perpetual little home-based business that is typical in today's small business population.

I'm not saying that everybody is going to become a billionaire business mogul. But why limit yourself? Why not keep your options open and let God bring you into your calling? Allow yourself to go as far as you can go. And, by having your eye on a longer-term objective you're more likely to be successful in the shorter term.

If you're not ready to make this key decision, it's okay and my sincere advice to you is to wait to finish this book. Pause here. You can save yourself a lot of time that you could be devoting to praying and preparing yourself mentally and emotionally for making your irrevocable decision. The word "irrevocable" means that you've made a decision you're fixed on and refuse to go back. It's irreversible, a done thing that you aren't going to question in the future when you face a few difficulties or uncertainties. If you are a Christian believer, it is REALLY important to look within yourself for the Holy Spirit to confirm for you what you ought to do both as to timing and content. Don't do this on your own. Stop here and wait for the witness of peace and life that can only come through Christ. With God in the lead all the way, success is assured![9]

Steps for Getting Started

From here on, the basic assumption are that you've made that irrevocable decision, that you won't be looking back and that you won't be putting limits on yourself. So, you

---
[9] 1 Corinthians 15:57, 2 Corinthians 2:14

can involve yourself in the following steps to your home-based business in 30 days or less:

1. The first thing to do SINCERELY is finish reading this book and keep going over it until you UNDERSTAND it. The essentials for eventual success are contained in this book. You are going to make mistakes and the world's business environment will have effects on your business activities you can't control. But if you can master and follow the contents of this book, you have a very high probability of success. Don't sell it short and don't gloss over any of its contents. Learn it and put it into action!

2. The second step if you haven't done so already is to decide on what you want to do from your home-based business. Most people will want to pursue something that comes to them naturally, something they're already interested in. Many people convert hobbies into profit-generating businesses. If you've had a long- time interest in a particular product or service, it could be pointing you toward something to pursue in business. People are more likely to succeed in business if they're working on something they're interested in and passionate about.

    Also, implement one that requires little or no startup capital (unless you've already accumulated the capital). If you need any significant amount of capital to start your new business, <u>the reality is that it's very</u>

<u>difficult to find unsecured commercial loans for new ventures</u>. Many people use credit cards and other forms of unsecured debt. Some even mortgage their homes to start their businesses. We strongly recommend <u>against</u> burdening a new home-based business and yourself with any kind of debt. If it seems that you do need to incur a lot of startup debt, it would be a sign for many people that it's either the wrong time or the wrong type of business. *To borrow against one's home to start a new business is especially something to be avoided.* In any event, most home-based businesses are started with an initial capitalization of less than five thousand dollars. And anyway, you want to risk as little as possible until your concept has been tested and proven.

At the end of this chapter, you will find for your consideration a list of the most popular home-based business ideas. Perhaps they will stimulate your thinking and help you ENVISION your idea. Every entrepreneur needs a VISION of what he/she is going to do in their business. The starter of a home-based business is a visionary who understands the function and purpose of the venture and can SEE the immediate next steps into the future. People who don't have a clear vision for what they're doing and going to have a much higher risk of failure. The Bible says that people should have a clear vision to obtain success in life.[10]

---

[10] Proverbs 29:18

3. The third step is to choose a name for your company. It should be something catchy that gets people's attention and communicates a sense of the service or benefit that a customer/client will receive by connecting to your company. It should be a name that no one else is using so you will need to verify that the name you want to use is available in your state's registry of business names. For most states that registry is in the hands of your Secretary of State and you can go on line or call the office of your Secretary to find out. This MUST be done and it's usually very easy to determine, less than five or ten minutes. There may be a small fee involved depending on the state.

   The name you choose also needs to work well on the Internet. So think about some URL names for your future website and go find one that's not taken already. There are free services available like Host Gator and Go Daddy. Keep in mind that your objective should be to come up with a name that's compatible with a Dot-Com URL address because as of the writing of this chapter, dot-com addresses are still the most popular. Stay with dot.com not matter what unless your home business will be something particular like lull-fledged ministry that customarily use dot-org addresses.

4. As soon as you decide on the name for your new business you will need to register it with your State's registration process. That is typically in the hands of

the Secretary of State. You may also need to register it in your county and/or municipality. You can call the offices of your local County Clerk and Municipal Clerk and ask if you ae required to register your new company. There may be a small related fee.

5. The next step is to open a bank account in the company name you have just finished registering. That name must already be registered with your state before the bank will be able to open your account. You want a separate bank account from your personal account(s) and you do NOT want to operate your new business from a bank account under your personal name. Get used to having separate bank accounts, private and business, and do NOT operate the business directly from a personal bank account. Keep the funds separate and the transactions at arms-length from each other. You can transfer funds back and forth but do NOT ever pay business bills directly from your personal bank account and do NOT ever pay personal bills directly out of your business account. You have no idea how important this paragraph is so follow it religiously! Keep in mind that you are preparing for bigger things in your future so start off right no matter how modest your initial home-based business is.

6. The next step is to write a SIMPLE business plan. I know you won't want to do this step so early in the process but it's one of those seemingly superfluous

administrative things that is actually highly essential. It's essential because it will help you clarify your VISION and I am very serious when I counsel here to get this VISION thing straight before you go forward with the operation of your business. You need to be able to write down a brief description of what your new business is going to do, what your purposes and objectives are both qualitative and quantitative.

I understand that people are eager to get started and want to skip over the administrative foundation building. But be sure of this: you have no idea how important the building of a strong foundation is. I can give you Scripture for it[11] and I can tell you from personal experience that you need to force yourself to stick to what works. One of the things that ALWAYS works is building a strong foundation. Therefore, DO sit down and do the best you can to WRITE your vision in the form of a business plan so that you will be implementing an established program.[12]

In the next chapter you will find a format for a simple business plan but there is also some additional information for more sophisticated plans in case your new business will start out further advanced than just a tax optimization idea. Just utilize there what you need. In sum, writing down plans and objectives is a key part of planning for success.

---

[11] Matthew 7:24-27
[12] Habakkuk 2:2-3

7. Step seven is to decide on the type of business structure you want to start with. Most new home-based businesses can and should start out as a Sole Proprietorship. The only reasons you would want to start with a more sophisticated type of organization are as follows:

   a. If your new company causes you to incur a substantial personal liability, you would need an LLC or a Corporation to protect yourself.

   b. If your new company will start out with a high income, you would want to consider other organization types to optimize your tax obligation. Consult with a CPA to make the right decision.

   Most people reading this book will be starting up a brand new home-based business from "scratch." So, you will only need a Sole Proprietorship type of organization. You will officially become a Sole Proprietor the moment you have completed the dual task of registering your company name with your Secretary of State and opening a bank account. That's all it takes and the more sophisticated organizations can be looked at more closely when you have begun to grow and succeed. For most home-based businesses the next level of organization will likely be an LLC or a Sub-Chapter S corporation. When the time comes, consult a CPA to make an informed decision taking into account your location, your type of business activity and the related liability.

8. Step number eight is to purchase a computer if you don't have one already and then put a basic website on line. Every business in America no matter how basic or new needs to have a website to establish credibility for the purpose of doing business. You may see yourself in the beginning as being small, but keep in mind that you're looking to the future for something bigger. SO GET A WEBSITE and show people you're in business for the long haul. You will then be operating your new business on a worldwide basis and you will be amazed at how many people will come in contact with your website. I will assume you already own a computer but in case you don't, you MUST purchase one even if you are only receiving emails on behalf of your company.

Your website doesn't have to be complicated and there are several ways to go about getting it on line. If possible, your website should actually be a blogsite. A blogsite is simply a website that is updated on a regular and frequent basis. The updates are usually informal and written in a conversational style that attracts the attention of a following that is interest in an ongoing topic-focus and/or the author.

Most people who blog swear that the place to go for your blog is www.wordpress.org because it has the greatest capability. Notice that the preferred place to go is dot-org and NOT dot-com. WordPress has the two places but you will want the dot-org so you can put your blog with a hosting company of your choice that accepts onsite advertising by third parties. If you have a Webmaster construct the blogsite for you it will cost perhaps $500.00. if you have some web skills I am told that you will be able to handle WordPress.org yourself with some education and preparation which is made available to you when you open your account. You could also open a hosting account with Host Gator.com and they will help you understand Word how to get set up in WordPress.com.

But since you are just starting out, you can begin your blogging with perhaps a simpler platform such as Blogger.com or Wix.com. Another suggestion is to open a hosting account with Go Daddy.com and try to answer your questions. They also have a free platform for constructing your own non-blogging website which even I was able to use successfully. And there are other companies you can consider but you should make your own online study because blog construction is really not our expertise.

9. Number nine is to purchase your office equipment and supplies and get ready to start your business. You want to ALWAYS be organized and prepared for future expansion and success. You need a comfortable and functional work station with a telephone and a computer. A printer-scanner will come in handy and you can find everything you need for less than $100.00. That's it! Don't forget to look at second-

hand office furniture stores, hand-me-down sources, Amazon.com, Goodwill or wherever comes to mind. You don't need much so keep the cost down.

10. Finally, for Step Ten I want you to consider purchasing an accounting system. You won't necessarily need it at the beginning but if you have it you break yourself in for the day in the not too distant future when you WILL definitely need it and may have to hire someone to run it for you in your office. The system to purchase to purchase is Quick Books Pro. The cost is about $200.00 and you will be entering your deposits and disbursements into the software on an ongoing basis. The software takes care of the accounting for you and at the end of the month will generate an Income Statement which you need to learn to understand and use on a monthly basis.

All you have to do to be successful is: (1) follow these ten steps exactly as they have been laid out for you, and (2) read and understand the rest of this book. It may not all apply now but it soon will. Keep going because you will eventually need the information that follows to keep your probability for success above 90 percent. This isn't a FAKE warning: YOU NEED THE INFORMATION THAT FOLLOWS. If you think you know it all already, please check it out anyway as a refresher course to be sure. I want you to succeed and tell everyone that it all started when you read this book.

TOP 55 IDEAS FOR SMALL BUSINESS STARTUPS[13]

Following is a list of the most popular small business ideas with an expected startup cost of less than $5,000. Use it to stimulate your thinking for your own company.

GROUP ONE:
<u>$1,500 or less to start up</u>

Accountant	Home Inspection
Boat Cleaning	Household Organizer
Bicycle Repair	Import/Export Specialist
Business Plan Service	Interior Decorator
Chimney Sweep	Jewelry Making
Cleaning Service	Marketing Copy Writer
Computer Repair	Notary
Consultant	Personal Concierge
Dog Breeder	Personal Trainer
EBay Assistant	Property Manager
Editorial Services	Small Engine Repair
Electronics Repair	Solar Energy Consultant
Event Planning	Tax Preparer
Expert Witness service	Taxidermist
Financial Planner	Upholstering
Flea Market	Used Book Sales
Golf Coach	
Home Energy Auditor	

---

[13] *https://www.entrepreneur.com/article/201588*

GROUP TWO:
$1,500 TO $3,000 to start up

Appliance Repair	Herbal Farm Stand
Computer Training	Landscaper
Desktop Publisher	Massage Therapist
Fence Installation	Moving Service
Freelance Graphics Designer	Music Lessons
Gift Basket Service	Photographer
Graffiti Removal	Rug Cleaning
Hairstylist	Website Developer

GROUP THREE:
$3,000 TO $5,000 to start up

Bed and Breakfast
Christmas Sales
Day Care
Pet Sitting

Certainly this isn't an exhaustive list but it should get you thinking. Compare this list to things you're passionate about or that occupy your thoughts or that might already involve you in some kind of hobby. Pray about it and ask the Lord what He wants you to do for the Kingdom. But before you start something, be SURE about what you want to do, sure enough to invest adequate time in getting yourself prepared for success.[14]

---

[14] Excerpted from: "55 Surefire Home Based Businesses You Can Start for Under $5,000." *By Entrepreneur Press & Cheryl Kimball (2009).*

6. Basics of Writing a Business Plan

Every business needs a written Business Plan even if you're not going to borrow money and even if you are starting out as a home-based business. If you *are* thinking about borrowing money, say for example to finance working capital, the first thing the bank will ask you for is your business plan. For small bank loans a simple three to five page Executive Summary of your Business Plan will usually be adequate for the typical small business and it should contain the basic information outlined at the end of this chapter. Home-based business owners need to know this info for the future so don't skip it. It's here especially for you.

If you want to get more sophisticated you can purchase software either on line or at your local office supply store. The related software purchase cost is on average about $150. There are also Business Plan provider/preparers including our own ministry with a normal cost at present of about $495 which includes ONGOING online access, mentoring and archiving. Our Business Plans can also uniquely interface with the QuickBooks Accounting system so the user can compare current performance against the Business Plan on an ongoing basis.

Other Business Plan providers charge $500-$750 not including online access nor ongoing mentoring nor the interface with QuickBooks. Here are a couple of websites outside our ministry (as of this writing) you can review:

www.businessplans.com
www.bizplaneasy.com

Having a Business Plan addresses the need to be organized but few small businesses actually do one. Most of the folks who DO are successful. The ones who are successful, like you want to be, can show you their Business Plans and they faithfully update them at least every year. Said another way, 90+% of small business failures don't have one. Your Plan doesn't have to be complicated either, so keep it simple and use it.

I also think it's very important for a small business to keep a close watch on a short list of near-term objectives. A good time to review your list of objectives is at the end of the year just before you start the new-year. Any objectives you didn't achieve in the previous year should be re-evaluated and either dropped or revised or retained and repeated for the coming operating period. I don't like to see organizations without a vibrant list of operating objectives with corresponding action plans that are under ongoing review and are constantly in motion.

When you get to the point of borrowing funds for your company, the lender will want a detailed accounting of what you'll be using the funds for. They will also want to know how the loan will affect your operating performance. In other words, what will be the results of borrowing the money compared to not borrowing? If the indebtedness doesn't improve your operating performance over the next three years verses NOT borrowing the funds, then the lender will want to know why you want to borrow. Pointless indebtedness isn't something lenders want to consider.

When you borrow funds, you will need to have your financial statements ready as attachments to the Business Plan. The financial statements have to include an Income Statement and a Balance Sheet. The Income Statement should show the current year performance and a forecast for the next three years. You will also need tax returns for the previous two or three years both personal and business. On the Balance Sheet the lender is going to want to see some liquidity that could pay back a substantial portion of the debt if it became necessary.

If you are borrowing for a small company with a relatively limited amount of business assets, be prepared to have to personally guarantee the repayment of the debt. That's just the way it is and it means that if your small business fails, you will have to use personal assets to repay the outstanding debts of the business. Or, the business will have to seek protective bankruptcy.

Another use for a Business Plan is for the purpose of attracting investors to provide additional capital for your business. Very often that type of Business Plan will be more detailed and you will need to be prepared to answer a lot of questions. You will also need to be prepared to give up equity in your company equivalent to taking in partners. I don't usually recommend soliciting investors who have to have an equity position in your company unless you can avoid having them participate in its management. By all means avoid that hassle if you can.

Most people think it's easy to borrow from the SBA (Small Business Administration). But it is NOT easy and involves a lengthy administrative process. If you are a new startup business, don't waste your time until you have at least 12 consecutive months of profitable operating performance. The SBA likes to see an established track record for young companies that are looking to expand.

When you do become a candidate for an SBA Loan, you will find a wealth of information in Appendix One of this publication that will help you apply for one. We can also assist you if the going gets tough. It's not an easy process.

In sum, a professionally prepared Business Plan serves three basic purposes:

1. Helps you get organized.
2. Provides essential information for prospective lenders.
3. Provides basis for monitoring operating performance.

In short, a Business Plan works like a financial plan or a budget that will really help you be successful. Please don't ignore it because you might be sorry.

The following page shows a functional outline of a very basic Business Plan. You can start with it and graduate to one of our more sophisticated online plans later whenever you're ready to graduate to the next level.

BUSINESS PLAN

Name of Company: _____
Plan Date: _____

Description and Purpose of the Business performed:

Basic Mission:

Principal Operating Objectives:

Financial Performance and Objectives:
    Last Year
    Current Year Forecast:
    Current Year +1:
    Current Year +2:

Current Year Operating Budget:
      Sales
      Cost of Goods Sold
      Gross Margin
      Operating Expenses
      Net Profit

Future Plans and Objectives:

Contact Information:

Names and Addresses of the Principals of the Business:

BE SURE TO DO YOUR RESEARCH

7. Types of Organizations

One of the questions you'll face as you start forming your new business is which type of organization you should use. Many small businesses start out as Sole Proprietorships and then graduate into a more sophisticated form after the business has proven itself. They can also start out in one of the other forms depending upon the circumstances.

None of them is particularly difficult to put together and most cities have specialized business formation agencies that can help you including making the appropriate registrations with your state for a relatively modest fee. There are also Internet firms that provide this service. It's important to make the right decision on which one of the following main types of organizations to choose:

1. **Sole Proprietorship** = A sole proprietorship is a type of business entity that is owned and run by one individual and in which there's no legal distinction between the owner and the business.

    The owner receives all profits (subject to taxation specific to the business) and has unlimited responsibility for all losses and debts. Every asset of the business is owned by the proprietor and all debts of the business are the proprietor's. It is a "sole" proprietorship in contrast with *partnerships* involving more than one owner.

As a Sole Proprietor of a registered business, you will be able to deduct certain business expenses for the purpose of reducing the amount you pay for income taxes even though you're still on the payroll as an employee of a large company. This is why we recommend that everybody try to have a registered small business conducting at the least some simple ongoing enterprise that meets IRS requirements.

2. **General Partnership** = Partnerships involve a business organization formed between two or more people. All the members are known as partners and are joint owners of the entire business organization. Let's be clear about this type of organization: if at all possible avoid it and find another way to start your small business. Analyze it: why do you need a partner other than your spouse?

Nevertheless, if you decide on getting into one, the partners as a group are accountable for any profit, loss or liability of the business organization. An important step for this type of company is that all partners need to enter into a formal, pre-defined written agreement regarding profit sharing and loss bearing, before starting their venture.

Irrespective of the amount of capital brought in by each of the various partners or the profit-loss sharing percentage agreed on for each partner in what's called a *General Partnership*, any partner can be legally liable to pay off the TOTAL debts of the company if there's a problem in the future because the partners have *joint* liability. There is also *several* liability in other types of partnerships which mean that their obligation for paying the debts of the organization is proportional to the capital they have contributed. Finally, it's imperative to have a specific *Agreement of Dissolution* in the event one of the Partners wants to leave.

One thing that's often overlooked with Partnerships is that there must also be a mutual agreement dealing with how business decisions are made. There should always be one of the partners who has the authority to make the final decision for the business entity when the voting of the partners is tied. Many partnerships have failed because the partners couldn't agree on some particular issue or other and was no longer able to go forward for lack of a key business decision.

3. **C-Type Corporation** = A traditional Corporation (or a "C" Corporation) is a business structure that is created as a separate, distinct legal entity from its owners (also called "shareholders"). Once a corporation is formed, the corporation can have its own bank accounts, own property, conduct business, and even establish a line of credit distinctly separated from the individual accounts or credit of the shareholders. The primary advantage to having a business formed as a corporation is the fact that the shareholders are not necessarily personally liable for the debts and legal liabilities incurred by the corporation. For example, if

a corporation is sued for business reasons and loses, the shareholders will not be required to satisfy the debts of the corporation from their own personal assets (<u>unless they have personally guaranteed those debts</u>). This safeguards assets and properties of the individual shareholders, and as such, is more attractive to potential investors.

Once a corporation is established, the shareholders must name (via an election process) a board of directors that's responsible for the operation of the business, making business decisions, and managing all business-related activities. This board is elected by the shareholders of the corporation, and once named, the board appoints "officers" of the corporation to specific duties. This usually includes a secretary, a treasurer, etc.

Another important thing to know about the formation and maintenance of a corporation is that certain corporate formalities must be observed. These are things like a required annual meeting of the board of directors, the necessity to maintain the corporate "minutes," the separation of corporate and personal funds (no "co-mingling" of funds), and a necessity to maintain written agreements for all corporate transactions (including internal transactions e.g. internal loans, executive compensation agreements, etc.).

4. **S-Type Corporation** = The name "S-Corporation" comes from the fact that its organization meets the

IRS requirements for taxation under *Subchapter S* of the IRS Tax Code. It's a corporation that is structured to provide a pass-through entity for tax purposes, much like a partnership whose income or losses "pass through" to the individual shareholders' personal tax returns (in direct proportion to their investment or ownership in the company), while still providing the same protections for assets and from liabilities as a traditional corporation. The shareholders will pay personal income taxes based on the S-Corporation's income, regardless of whether or not the income is actually distributed, but they will avoid the "double taxation" that has to be paid in connection with the traditional "C" Corporation which includes: (a) a tax must be paid on corporate profits plus (b) the shareholders pay tax on any dividend distributions they receive. The S-Type Corporation can be particularly attractive to the small family business where limited liability is a particular concern.

Most small businesses starting out will probably want to move quickly from the Sole Proprietorship organization to an S-corporation. Anyone who's still working as an employee of a big company can conduct their own S-type corporation as a side small business and take advantage of the business deductions the same as a Sole Proprietorship. Get some help from a CPA to identify legal deductions that are available to small businesses.

5. **Limited Liability Company** = An LLC is a hybrid business entity having certain characteristics of both a corporation and a partnership. An LLC is a type of unincorporated association and is therefore not a corporation. The primary characteristic an LLC shares with a corporation is limited liability and the primary characteristic it shares with a partnership is the availability of pass-through income taxation. It is often more flexible than a corporation and can have a single owner.

   LLC members are subject to the same liability protection as corporate shareholders. However, it's more difficult to pierce the LLC veil because LLCs don't have many formalities to maintain as corporations. So long as the LLC and its members don't commingle funds, it's difficult to pierce its veil. Membership interests in LLCs and partnership interests also have a significant level of protection through the charging order mechanism. The charging order limits the creditor of a debtor-partner or debtor-member to the debtor's share of distributions without conferring on the creditor any voting or management rights. LLC members may in certain circumstances also incur a personal liability in cases where distributions to members render the LLC insolvent.

To sum up, the purpose of this chapter is to introduce you to the knowledge that there are several kinds of organizations you can consider. Your best approach when you start your new business is to contact a CPA in order to receive current and direct advice on the type of organization you should choose in relation to specifically what you have in mind.

Nevertheless, you can start any small business almost immediately simply by registering a DBA in your state and opening a bank account. Then you can change later to another business type once you've become established.

Most people will wind up in an S-Corporation either from the start or later on after a time as a Sole Proprietor. Keep in mind that the formation of any corporation including an S-Type is a process that you'll probably need some help with. And, it requires a bit more administrative knowledge than a Sole Proprietorship.

To end this chapter, we want to emphasize the importance of establishing a good relationship with a CPA or an experienced business accountant. Do NOT try to cheap out on this because <u>we ALL need expert PROFESSIONAL advice to be successful</u>. Keep that in mind: you WILL need professional assistance and to try skipping it is a formula for disaster. Along with that, don't try to prepare your own business tax returns either. You won't do it correctly and you won't have time to learn what you need to know to do them correctly. PLEASE: never cheap out on the financial and administrative parts of your business!

Relative Advantages and Disadvantages of Various Business Forms

Issue	Sole Proprietorship	C Corp.	General / Limited Liability Partnership	Limited Partnership	Limited Liability Company	S Corp.
Self-employment Income from Entity	Yes	No	Yes	Yes -GP No -LP	Usually; See Proposed Regs§ 1.140-2(a)-18	To extent of salary and bonus
Effect of Passive Loss Limitation Rules	N/A	Applies at corp. level/generally avoidable for larger corps.	Partners may or may not materially participate	Ltd. partners deemed not to materially participate	Members may or may not materially participate	Shareholders may or may not materially participate
Availability of Entity Losses to Owners	N/A	No	Flow through of losses to owners	Flow through of losses to owners	Flow through of losses to owners	Flow through of losses to owners
Fringe Benefits	Limited compared to C Corp	Widest available	Limited compared to C Corp	Limited compared to C Corp	Limited compared to C Corp	Limited compared to C Corp
Estate Planning Opportunities	Fair	Very good	Good	Very good	Very good	Fair
Accumulated Earnings and PHC Tax	N/A	Section 531 and Section 541 applicable	No	No	No	No
State Taxes	Same as individual	Generally uniform and deductible	Generally uniform	Generally uniform	States vary	States vary
Dividend Received Deduction	N/A	Allowed	Not allowed	Not allowed	Not allowed	Not allowed
Effect of Bus. Liabilities on Owner's Basis	Full effect	No effect	Proportionate share	Limited partners share in nonrecourse	Proportionate share	Only shareholder's own loans
Alternative Minimum Tax	Subject to AMT	Subject to corporate AMT	Preference items flow to each partner	Preference items flow to each member	Preference items flow to each member	Preference items flow to each shareholder
Method of Accounting	Cash method	Depends on size and ownership	Generally may use cash method	Generally may use cash method	Generally may use cash method unless farming syndicate	Generally may use cash method

Source: Principles of Ag Law, Roger A. McEowen, Neil E. Harl

8. How to Build Startup Credit

Are you thinking about using credit to help finance your new business? You're not alone because statistics show that over 65% of all business owners use credit for things that have to be purchased by the business. But what's somewhat alarming about that is that only 50% of those credit accounts are actually in the name of the business. In other words, they are personal accounts <u>in the name of the owner or a spouse</u>.

As a business owner, using personal credit cards for business is a risky practice since you assume total liability personally. If your company is sued or fails financially, you risk losing personal assets and your good credit rating. So try to avoid it and do your best to NOT use your personal assets as collateral for business credit.

So how do you go about building credit in the company's name without putting your personal credit on the line? For starters, if you're already operating as a sole proprietorship, you'll need to incorporate your business so you can obtain a *Federal Tax Identification number*. It's often referred to as an EIN Number. If you're just starting up, then go directly to an S-Type Corporation and skip the sole proprietorship model.

As a corporation your company is treated as a separate entity with its own tax registration with the IRS and state agencies and it's totally separated from you personally. It files its own tax returns and it can also create its own credit lines completely separate from its owners. Banks will ask you for a personal guarantee for bank loans but what we're talking about in this section is building startup credit with either corporate credit cards or trade credit so you can avoid bank loans.

Your company's Tax ID Number aka *Employer Identification Number (EIN)* is the number that you will use to register with the business credit bureaus including *Dun and Bradstreet, Credit Safe, Capital One Business, Experian, Equifax,* etc.

You will also be required to provide your EIN number on corporate credit applications because lenders use this information to conduct a business credit check on your company before deciding whether or not to extend a line of credit to it.

Before you start applying for credit, make sure your corporate records, state filings and required business licenses are all up to date. In addition, get your company's phone number listed in the 411 directory so a supplier or lender can complete every aspect of its verification during the underwriting process.

After that you should be ready to apply for credit and the best place to start is with your supplier-vendors. Many types of suppliers, including major brands, extend lines of credit to businesses like yours giving you the opportunity to finance inventory purchases and conserve your company's cash. You may start with a vendor with short-term credit say like 15 days, but with good experience most vendors will soon be open to the idea of extending your credit repayment term to longer periods like 30 or 60 days. And don't forget that most of your vendors have competitors who may be more than willing to extend credit terms to your company in order to win your business. Credit is often a good way to secure new business for them. And, when YOU give credit to your customers, use the related Accounts Receivable as collateral for bank loans and avoid a personal guarantee.

You should focus on applying for credit with suppliers that provide products and services your company needs regularly so that you can make the related purchases with your credit lines. You can usually obtain products like office supplies, computers and marketing materials with payment terms ranging from net 30 to net 60 days.

By paying all your invoices on time, you'll be building good business credit history which will increase your company's credit rating and make it possible to obtain additional financing as time goes on. Ask your vendors to be sure and report your good credit payment history to the commercial credit bureaus because they're the ones who assemble and publish the related credit reports.

With a strong business credit report you can stop relying on your personal guarantee for the financing that your company needs. Since a creditor, lender or supplier will be able to easily determine your company's risk level by contacting the commercial credit bureaus, qualifying for future credit will be an increasingly easier process.

As a new startup, it's certainly possible for you to decide on operating your business as a sole proprietorship and using your personal credit to fund your business simply because it's one of the easiest structures to create and you already have credit cards on hand. If you're operating your business as simply a tax shelter and you aren't interested in making it grow yet, you can consider staying as a sole proprietor.

But if you want to grow your business more quickly by building business credit, you can improve your company's image, protect your personal credit, limit your liability and increase your credit capacity since businesses once they're established can obtain typically 10 to 100 times greater financing then an individual.

A Word of Caution

You will most likely discover that it's relatively easy to obtain credit for your company especially as time goes on and you demonstrate your ability to pay your bills on time. But there's a tremendous temptation in front of you which is getting too much credit. Many of the business failures racked up in the first five years of life are caused by obtaining more credit than the company can afford.

When banks evaluate companies as prospective borrowers, they will tend to look at various operating and financial ratios calculated from data you will provide them on your company's financial statements. One of the traditional ratios is called the *Current Ratio* and it's calculated as follows: current assets divided by current liabilities as reported on your company Balance Sheet. If the ratio is less than one, it indicates to the creditor that you don't have enough assets to pay off all your short-term debts. A ratio more than three might suggest to the bank that your company isn't being aggressive enough. Therefore, the traditional view for this ratio is that it should be more than one and perhaps not much greater than two. You accountant can provide you with this ratio on a monthly basis if you request it and you should use it just for a basic indication of the financial health of your company.

In addition, banks and accountants use a number of other ratios to evaluate the financial health of a business. Your accountant can educate you about the ones that are the most popular for the industry that your company is involved in and some related guidelines. But the basic concept is this: it's generally okay to increase your accounts payable to your vendors up to just BEFORE you have to start struggling to pay them ALL on time. If you have to start asking vendors for extended repayment terms, you've waited too long and acquired too much debt or you've experienced an unexpected financial hiccup that's telling you to start reducing accounts payable until you're not struggling anymore. Generally, you shouldn't owe more to your suppliers than you could pay off if you had to suddenly shut down your business tomorrow.

Another point to bring up in this section is that the tendency to over-borrow and have trouble paying creditors on time is often related to the owner-entrepreneur taking too much money out of the business for compensation USUALLY in combination with granting too much credit to the company's customers. How do we avoid these temptations?

First, you need to put yourself on a regular salary so that the company is *planning* for your compensation and then resist the temptation to take out additional money when you have an unexpected personal need that arises. What would you do if you were working for someone else and that personal need arose? You would probably use a personal credit card to take care of that need and then repay the credit card debt over a period of time from the ongoing compensation you're receiving from your employer. Get in the habit of working the same way with your own company.

The other big problem is the temptation to grant more credit to your customers than you can afford. Most entrepreneurs are way better sales people than they are administrators. They will do whatever's necessary to make a sale. But here's the problem: if you grant too much credit you won't have enough cash on hand when it comes to replenish your inventory or pay your ongoing operating bills! You made the sale but you don't benefit from it until you collect the payment from the customer and put the revenue back into your business.

These are some of the factors that lead to business failure. The moral of the story is this: JUST BE CAUTIOUS and don't overdo the indebtedness of your company! It can be a good thing to use other people's money but keep it where you can pay it off if you have to and don't be using other people's money to create a higher lifestyle for yourself. Debt is strictly for the purpose of helping your business grow and expand. Otherwise, AVOID IT!

Also, don't be in a hurry to give too much credit to make a sale. Find out what industry practices are for your type of business and stick to that guideline. If a customer starts having trouble paying you on time you need to be on top of that and be quick to reduce your exposure. Keep this in mind: it is ALWAYS better to NOT make a sale than to make a bad sale you can't collect on.

9. Other Essential Financial Issues

There are several other financial subjects we ought to go over before you go off to start your new business. Remember that I told you in an earlier chapter that the financial part of your new business will be the most important even though the operating part is more fun. I repeat it here and emphasize the following: YOU <u>MUST</u> AGGRESSIVELY PURSUE A BASIC UNDERSTANDING OF THE FINANCIAL PART OF YOUR BUSINESS.

Accounting

The first subject is the importance of keeping your accounting up to date. In the beginning you can make the entries yourself and then later on hire a bookkeeper to keep things up to date. It's very important to do this as you go along so you don't come to the end of a tax year with a cardboard box full of papers and receipts that you'll have to pay someone to get organized for you.

I personally like the *Intuit Quick Books* accounting system because it can fit almost any business scenario. You will probably need some instruction but there are plenty of community workshops you can attend, and also QB has some tutorials that will teach you the principles of basic accounting. You CAN do this if you can learn to enter simple income and expense items and from there the system will pretty much take care of itself for entry level accounting. But you must have somebody on top of this part of your business so it's kept up to date monthly.

I also like the online version of QB because it's ongoing, your historical information is readily available and it's all backed up on QB servers. The other advantage of QB online is that it updates automatically so you don't have to buy the updates every year. The only downside is that you will have to pay a monthly user fee of about $25 to $30 but it's really worth it. If you get a CPA to open your account for you as one of their clients, you will probably get to enjoy a substantial discount.

Before leaving this section I want to leave you with a couple of accounting basics. The first is that a successful small business needs three principal financial statements.

Income Statement

The first is an *Income Statement* containing the following major categories:

- *Sales Revenue*
- *Less Cost of the products sold (aka Direct Costs)*
- *Equals Gross Revenue*
- *Less Operating Expenses*
- *Equals Net Profit before Taxes*

An *Income Statement* tells you from month-to-month whether or not you're making any money. Most small business people have no idea. They can tell you everything about sales and nothing about finances. You need to know on an urgent ongoing basis whether or not your business is profitable. Otherwise you'll probably fail.

Balance Sheet

The second major financial statement is called a *Balance Sheet*. It is called that because the value of every business is evaluated by two equal sides of an equation:

Total Assets = Liabilities + New Worth

The *Balance Sheet* tells the user the value of your company on the date it's prepared. The value of your business is called its *Net Worth*. It's also important to look at this financial statement over a period of several years to determine the trend. Is the *Net Worth* of your small business trending up or down? If it's going down it tells the user that your liabilities are increasing faster than your assets which could be an unhealthy trend.

Cash Flow Statement

The third major financial statement is called a *Cash Flow Statement*. Its primary purpose is to provide information about a company's cash receipts and cash payments. Cash flow is NOT the same as net income; it's about the movement of money into and out of your company. The cash flow statement reports the cash provided and used by the operating, investing, and financing activities of a company during a particular accounting period. Information used to prepare a cash flow statement is taken from the income statement for the current year and balance sheets for the past two years.[15]

---

[15] https://www.zionsbank.com/pdfs/biz_resources_book-4.pdf

At the end of this chapter you'll find UNRELATED examples of these three financial statements. Study until you understand them. Most small business owners do NOT understand these business basics which is the main reason why 75% of them will fail before they're five years old. In other words, Small Business owners keep trying to be lazy and uninformed about small business financial administration and it doesn't work out 75% of the time.

Taxes

I also want to emphasize the importance of keeping your taxes up to date because I continually run across self-employed entrepreneurs who're behind in filing their tax returns. Please don't do that! You have a LEGAL obligation to be current and orderly about the reporting and payment of your taxes. Render unto Caesar what is Caesar's and be glad that you made enough income that you owe a few tax dollars. And, NEVER allow yourself to get behind in the filing of your returns. Even if something happens and you don't have enough money for the moment to pay the tax you owe, it's usually better to go ahead and file your returns and send the related payment later with a little interest added on.

Most small business people will have a Form 1040 to file that summarizes personal income plus a Form 1120 for your S-corporation or the appropriate form for whatever business entity you finally adopted. If you collect Sales Tax, you will have to file and pay those tax receipts according to the procedures established in your state which is usually a monthly filing. If you have employees you will have to collect and account for the related payroll taxes. Or you can hire independent contractors and avoid the payroll tax situation. But, you will have to find out about the law and whether or not the people in your situation fit the legal profile for independent contractors.

When you start making some money, you really should hire an experienced tax accountant. Many of them have bookkeeping services so that your accountant can handle both requirements for you. They will keep track for you of when you have to file which tax return. It is unfortunate that taxes in our country have become so complicated but they are and you will need an expert. Do NOT begrudge the dollars you pay your accountant because he or she is performing a critical service that you are most likely NOT qualified to fully carry out on your own.

Now the idea of starting a small business in order to reduce you tax bill is so important that you'll find it discussed separately in a later chapter. The idea is that everyone should own a small business for the purpose of tax optimization.

Insurance

Finally, resist the temptation to be underinsured. If you employ trade workers, go ahead and pay your Workmen's Comp Insurance and don't try to cheap out on your people. You also need liability insurance, coverage on the risk on any inventory you are holding, insurance on your vehicles, medical insurance, etc. Many small business people carry an umbrella policy that provides an array of different coverages with one policy. Consult your insurance professional to find out the best solutions for your particular needs.

If you have a family you should also look into two types of special insurance coverage: one is called Key Man Insurance which would provide your family with income if you are temporarily unable to work in your business and the income you get from it is dependent on your ability to work. A related kind of insurance is Disability Insurance which provides income to your family if you are seriously disabled for an extended period of time and have to hire someone to take over your responsibilities.

Don't forget to have a generous life insurance policy with a payout on your life of at least ten times your annual earnings. Term insurance is okay especially if you're still young. But you should also try to save some of your profit and invest it into low-risk growth instruments that will help you safely increase the value of your estate over an extended period of time. Consult a qualified life insurance agent or estate planner for guidance.

In conclusion, the success or failure of a business is almost always financial. It can fail for various reasons but the failure is ALWAYS a financial conclusion. Therefore, it makes sense to pay attention to the financial condition of your company. You neglect it at your own risk.

MONTHLY BUSINESS BUDGET PERFORMANCE

Company Name: _____ Date: _____

EXPENSE CATEGORIES	BUDGET	ACTUAL	YEAR TO DATE

Employee Salaries
Payroll Taxes & Benefits
Consultants
Rent/Lease Payments
Mortgage Payments
Advertising/Promotions
Websites
Postage/Shipping
Supplies
Communications/Telephone
Utilities
Other Taxes
Insurance
Interest Expense
Bank Service Charges
Repairs & Maintenance
Professional Services-Acctg
Professional Services-Other
Travel & Entertainment
Miscellaneous

Total Monthly Operating Costs

(This is a basic operating form that successful businesses look at on a monthly basis. You want to have a financial plan going into the month and you want to you will want to know each month how you perform vs. your budget)

Note: the following three financial statements are NOT related:

EXAMPLE OF A TYPICAL SMALL BUSINESS INCOME STATEMENT

Period Covered: _____

	Total revenue	$	1,000,000	100%
Less	Cost of Goods Sold	$	426,200	42.6%
	Gross Profit	$	**573,800**	57.4%
Less	**Operating Expenses**			
	Accounting and legal fees	$	11,700	
	Advertising	$	15,000	
	Depreciation	$	38,000	
	Electricity	$	2,700	
	Insurance	$	15,200	
	Interest and bank charges	$	27,300	
	Postage	$	1,500	
	Printing and stationery	$	8,700	
	Professional memberships	$	1,800	
	Rent for premises	$	74,300	
	Repairs and maintenance	$	21,100	
	Training	$	6,900	
	Vehicle operating costs	$	20,000	
	Wages and salaries	$	223,500	
	Workers compensation	$	6,500	
	All other expenses	$	14,100	
Less	**Total Operating Expenses**	$	488,300	**48.8%**
Equals	**Net Profit**	$	**85,500**	**8.6%**

EXAMPLE OF A TYPICAL SMALL BUSINESS BALANCE SHEET

Date _____

ASSETS

    Current Assets

Cash	$ 20,000
Accounts receivable	$ 15,000
Inventory	$ 150,000
Total Current Assets	**$ 185,000**

    Non-Current Assets

Plant and equipment	$ 50,000
Business premises	$ 650,000
Vehicles	$ 70,000
Total Non-Current Assets	**$ 770,000**

TOTAL ASSETS   **$ 955,000**

    Current Liabilities

Accounts payable	$ 25,000
Bank overdraft	$ 10,000
Credit card debt	$ 5,000
Tax liability	$ 30,000
Total Current Liabilities	**$ 70,000**

    Non-Current Liabilities

Long term business loan 1	$ 450,000
Long term business loan 2	$ 50,000
Total Non-Current Liabilities	**$ 500,000**

TOTAL LIABILITIES   **$ 570,000**

NET ASSETS   **$ 385,000**

OWNERS EQUITY   **$ 385,000**

10. How to Minimize Personal Indebtedness

Now there is one particular piece of financial advice that deserves one whole chapter. The truth is this: you'll NOT get very far owning your own business if you put yourself in a lot of PERSONAL debt. You should avoid it like the plague and endeavor to pay everything off every month. Even in your business don't just get married to some credit line with an ongoing long-term balance paying only the interest every month. Before you know it that balance will become a permanent problem. Pay off your debts as soon as you can, ALWAYS.

If you're already in some amount of PERSONAL debt I want to counsel you in the remainder of this chapter about what you need to know to get out of it in the shortest possible time.

In order to be successful in implementing a Debt Elimination Plan, you need to be determined and you need to follow a *structured strategy*. Most people just try to throw money at their indebtedness without having a real plan that's based on sound reasoning. You need to implement YOUR reduction plan following certain steps that almost always work. You must be organized, you must be persistent, you must be consistent and you can't let anything hinder you from obtaining your ultimate objective. If you're fed up with indebtedness, if you're tired of always being restricted financially from what you want to do then you're about ready to go forward with this program.

Follow a Structured Strategy:

Step 1: Make an IRREVERSIBLE decision for your family that you're going to make a change and that you're going to follow your plan no matter what happens until you get out of debt. You must first decide to do something and take action before you can actually do it! But the decision to do it needs to be irreversible in the sense that you've made the decision not ever to go back to where you were. No going back! The decision has been made and you and your family are committed.

Step 2: Conduct a family meeting and get everyone on the same page. All the members of your family need to be in agreement with what you've decided to do and what your ultimate objective is. Make debt repayment a top priority for your WHOLE family. You need everyone involved, everyone committed to supporting your debt repayment plan. The entire family will have to make sacrifices until your objectives have been achieved and you need to be in agreement.

A good idea is to set up a procedure for resolving expenditure questions when they arise. From the beginning of the plan's implementation everybody should be in agreement on the procedure and how it will be used when these questions arise. Suppose one family member wants to spend money on something and the alternative is to apply that extra cash to your debt repayment plan. How will you resolve it without straining relationships? How will you be consistent when these questions keep coming up over the life of your program? You need a resolution procedure and you should agree from the beginning on how you'll use it.

And it's good to have children involved in the program too, even small children so that everybody is on board and totally supportive of the family project.

Step 3: The next step is to take the time to prepare a Family Budget. A simple form has been provided for your use at the end of this publication. Did you know that more than 85% of all American families have NEVER had a Family Budget? As the money comes it's spent according to a loose priority list that leaves open the family's optional expenses are going to be paid for. This is why most families run out of cash around the 21st of the month and have to put the rest of the month's expenses on credit cards. They have no idea or plan for how they're going to spend their money and so they just spend it until it runs out.

In order for this program to work you'll HAVE to have some form of Family Budget because part of the plan is to identify the amount of SURPLUS cash you're going to have available at the end of the month to apply to your debt repayment in the manner revealed in this publication. If you find yourself needing help in putting your Family Budget together, we recommend that you purchase one of our other publications, which provides a lot of detailed information about budgeting.

Step 4: From the outset of your program, you need to STOP using credit cards and STOP acquiring new debt. Cut those credit cards up if you have to and throw away the pieces! If you run short of cash during the month, do your best to find it in some other place in your Family Budget instead of using credit. If you don't stop acquiring new indebtedness, then you'll just be replacing the old debts with new ones. And you'll have less cash available to pay down your already existing debts because you'll be making new minimum payments on the new debt you've been acquiring. THIS PROGRAM CANNOT SUCCEED IF YOU DON'T STOP ACQUIRING NEW DEBT. Please take this step.

Step 5: As soon as possible put together a contingency fund of at least $2,000.00 <u>before</u> you start trying to get into your debt repayment program. If you get started in the repayment program too soon and an unexpected emergency strikes, it will be really discouraging to have to go back and take some of your old debt back to cover the problem. Having a contingency fund of this size can help you avoid that kind of dilemma. You will want to have those funds set aside in some kind of account that you can't access too easily and it should be a real emergency that causes you to go into your contingency.

Ultimately you will want to be saving for a much larger contingency fund as you're able of at least 6 months gross income and after that you should be working to put together a fully funded contingency fund of at least $100,000.00. That's one hundred thousand dollars! If you don't have debt payments every month you'll be surprised at how fast you can accumulate such a meaningful savings. Once you have it you'll probably never miss sleep again.

Step 6: Next you'll want to gather all your bills together. Find the most recent statement for each creditor that you won't be able to pay off at the end of the current month. Then arrange those statements starting with the lowest balance on top and going through all your creditors in the order of ascending outstanding balance until you reach the creditor with the highest outstanding balance at the end. For most families the creditor with the highest outstanding balance will be their home mortgage. To clarify: arrange all your debts from lowest outstanding balance at the top of the list to highest outstanding balance at the bottom.

On a piece of paper list your creditors from lowest outstanding balance to the highest. Indicate the creditor name, the current outstanding balance and the related monthly minimum payment. Section 3 has a table showing a typical scenario. This list will be the launch pad for your Accelerated Debt Repayment Plan

Step 7: Before you start the plan, pull your credit reports from the three national credit bureaus: Equifax, Experian and Trans Union. According to federal law you are entitled to receive one free credit report from each of the credit bureaus each year. To obtain your free annual credit report go to the following web site: **www.annualcreditreport.com**. You can order all three credit bureaus from this one web site.

The reason for ordering your credit reports is to be sure that you are including all your creditors in your debt reduction program. Sometimes people forget about older debts and will neglect to include them in the program. But your credit reports are likely to include everything up to seven years from the date of last activity. Don't forget to check the credit reports of both husband and wife because sometimes you can find a surprise where you didn't expect it. By the way, did you know that it's estimated that more than 70% of all credit reports contain errors? If your reports have any, you'll want to begin a correction process because as you go through your debt reduction program, you'll want to see improvement in your FICO Scores so you can obtain lower interest rates on your remaining debts and shorten the term of your repayment.

Step 8: Last, call each of your creditors and ask them to reduce your current interest rate to the lowest possible level. Many people who've made their payments on time and have generally a good payment history are paying interest rates higher than they have to because they haven't paid attention. Many Creditors will work with you and reduce your interest rate on a provisional basis but you have to request a reduction. If you make your payments on time for the next several months, they'll then consider another reduction. The point is though consumers have to be attentive and be proactive about their credit matters. You don't have to be afraid of your creditors. Tell them what you want and see what happens. The worst that could happen is that your creditor refuses to reduce your interest rate. But some of them WILL respond to your request and that could shorten your repayment program substantially because more of your monthly payments will be going to pay off principle. It's definitely worth a try!

If you feel the least bit intimidated by contacting your creditors, we recommend that you consider purchasing one of our other publications, which provides a lot of detailed information about how to deal with creditors. Just look for the following title in the publication list of Make a Way Ministries:

How to Work with Creditors Yourself When You're Facing a Payment Problem

Now you're ready to get started with your program. Take control of your finances, implement your repayment plan and stay on top of things. You'll be seeing substantial progress in no time!

Use the Low Balance Accelerator Approach

The key getting out of debt in the shortest possible time is to put the maximum amount of surplus cash into the program. Therefore, when you prepare your Family Budget form, you'll want to be tough and frugal in calculating the maximum amount of Surplus Cash you have left over after paying for all your living expenses. Look for money everywhere! You must be able to come up with a positive number for the Surplus Cash Calculation in order to get out of debt with this program.

Next, take the list of creditors and outstanding balances that you prepared above in Step 5 and add up all the monthly minimum payments. Then subtract the total of the monthly payment minimums from the available **Surplus Cash** that you derived from the preparation of your Family Budget. The resulting number is called the **Accelerator**.

Next, review your list of outstanding debts which you previously arranged starting with the one with the lowest balance and proceeding through the list to the creditor with the highest outstanding balance at the bottom of the list. Please see the Typical Example shown at the end of this section to help guide you through this exercise.
Your first objective is to ATTACK the debt with the lowest balance and pay it off first as explained below and then afterwards descending down the list as you pay off each creditor with the lowest balance.

As the final step, add the full **Accelerator** amount to the monthly minimum payment at the top of the priority list and do that every month until it's paid off. The top of the priority list is the one with the LOWEST outstanding balance. All the other bills receive just their normal minimum monthly payments.

When the top priority bill is paid off, i.e. the one with the lowest balance, calculate a new **Accelerator** by adding the monthly minimum of the bill you've just paid off to the old **Accelerator**. Then move this new **Accelerator** down to the second bill on the priority list adding it to the normal minimum payment you're already paying. Continue moving down the list in this manner applying an increasing **Accelerator** to each monthly minimum until the entire list of debts, INCLUDING YOUR MORTGAGE, has been totally paid off. If you ever receive extra money for something, always pay down the creditor with the lowest balance.

Using this approach you won't care which accounts have the highest interest rates because there's no significant difference in the repayment time between this approach and one that features a prioritization by interest rates. When we run the two different approaches through the computer, they always come out about the same. The advantage of the approach based on lowest outstanding balance is that you'll begin to see progress earlier which motivates most families to push through to victory.

That's the main reason we recommend it over the approach based on interest rates.

On the following pages you'll find an example of a simple accelerated repayment plan covering seven unsecured creditors. The secured debts (the mortgage on the home and the car note) have been included at the end of the list. This is a fairly typical example both in the number of creditors and the amount that the family is in debt. Please be sure to study the comments that follow the numbers until you're sure you understand how it works.

Then you're ready to design your own program. Make a list of all your creditors from lowest balance to highest and go for it!

Typical Example:

Creditor	Balance	Min Mo Payment
Discover	1,050	21
Sears	2,250	50
Citibank	3,000	68
Chase	3,500	70
Amex	4,200	84
Bank One	5,600	112
Capital One	6,100	183
Sub Total Unsecured	25,760	588
GMAC Auto	17,125	350
First Mortgage	153,200	1,250
TOTALS	**$196,025**	**$ 2,188**

EXPLANATIONS:

- Surplus Cash from Budget = 650 (before payments to unsecured creditors)
- Accelerator = 650 − 588 = 62 per month
- Accelerator should be added to the minimum payment at the top of the Priority list only
- Payment to Discover = 21 + 62 = 83 per month
- All other payments remain the same (i.e. pay only the minimum monthly payments) until Discover is paid off
- Then payment to Sears = 50 + 83 = 133 per month until paid off
- Then payment to Citibank = 68 + 133 = 201 per month until paid off, etc.

MONTHLY FAMILY BUDGET

INCOME

	Husband	Wife
Gross Wages		
Net Wages		
1099 Earnings		
Other Investments		
Alimony/Child Spt.		
Pension/Soc. Sec.		
Other		

EXPENSES

Tithe/Donation		Groceries	
Rent (incl. storage)		Lunches	
Mortgage		All Phones	
2nd Mtg/Equity Loan		Internet	
Property Taxes		TV/Cable	
Property Insurance		Car Payment (1)	
Condo/HOA Fees		Car Payment (2)	
Electricity/Gas		Auto Insurance	
Water/Sewer/Garbage		Auto Repair/Oil	

Gasoline/Tolls		Clubs/Hobbies	
Vacation Lodging		Subscriptions	
Ticket/Fare/Travel		Tobacco	
Clothing		Gifts	
Health Insurance		Cleaning/Laundry	
Doctor/Dentist		Hair/Person Care	
Meds/Vitamins		Pet Care	
School Tuition		Alimony/Child Spt.	
Books		Life Insurance	
Child Care		Savings/Investing	
Entertainment/ Dining		Misc/Other	

- Property Taxes and Homeowners Insurance should not be itemized if the mortgage payment includes the related escrows. If the mortgage payment does not cover taxes and insurance, those costs must be itemized where provided by dividing the annual total by 12 to equal a monthly allocation.
- Items such as car repairs, vacations, clothes and gift expenses can be calculated by dividing the annual total by 12 to equal a monthly allocation.

TOTAL COMBINED INCOME =

TOTAL EXPENSES =

AVAILABLE SURPLUS TO PAY DEBT =

Considerations for Your Personal Credit Reports

As you pay off your accounts you'll need to be aware of the effects of this program on your credit reports. It would be normal to assume that as you pay off your accounts it would be GOOD for your credit reports and increase all your FICO Scores. Well, it depends and that's why we've included this section in this publication. You'll need excellent FICO Scores if you ever need an emergency short-term loan.

First of all as you pay off an account your natural tendency will be to close the account even though you've hopefully put the related credit card somewhere out of your reach. But wait a minute: if the account you want to close is an older line of credit, older than say 3 or 4 years, it will be better for your credit scores to keep the account open with a zero balance. Having older lines of credit that are well managed are GOOD for your FICO Scores.

If you want to close something, close the newer accounts first. The lines of credit you obtained within the last 2 years or so can be closed first and you can save the older accounts for later. For closing accounts you want to have a gradual approach closing open accounts slowly over time working from newest to oldest. At the end of the program you should wind up with at least 3 open accounts, the older the better. Why 3 accounts? Because if you ever want to obtain a home mortgage the Lender is going to want to see at least 3 active trade lines on your credit reports in order to qualify you for the mortgage. In sum, don't overdo it. We're working under a flawed financial system so we need to be shrewd to make the best of it.

Another thing you should know is that it's good for your FICO to use your trade lines frequently. The trick is to know how to do that without getting into debt again. What you do is charge something on your credit cards during the month but pay it off totally at the end of the month. The credit reports will soon show the activity and as long as the outstanding balance is never greater than 40% of the account credit limit, the better your credit rating will be. In other words, it's better for your FICO Scores to show a little credit activity going through your open accounts than no activity at all. The fact that you're paying them off at the end of the month isn't reflected on your credit reports. If your credit reports show that you're operating with small balances in your open accounts, the computer models that determine the FICO Scores will interpret that as well-managed indebtedness which results in higher scores than no credit activity at all.

If any of your debts were settled for less than the outstanding balance of record, you will need to obtain a Satisfaction Letter from your Creditor that you can send to the Credit Bureaus to document your repayment. Satisfaction Letters should be obtained from the creditor BEFORE you pay the amount of the settlement. When you're dealing with creditors everything should be in writing. If you have any concerns about Debt Settlements, contact the Ministry office for advice: (800) 357-4223.

Also you may want to consider purchasing one of our other publications that deals with the task of improving your credit rating. Just look for the following title on Amazon.com:

Credit Repair that Reduces Monthly Payments

If you find yourself needing help in putting your Family Budget together, we recommend that you purchase one of our other publications, which provides a lot of detailed information about budgeting. Just look for the following title at Amazon.com:

Budgeting Yourself to Financial Victory

These publications have been successfully used for many years and can be a big help for most families. They are also not very expensive! If you don't like them, send them back to us for a full refund.

11. Setting Aside Cash Reserves

One of the biggest problems small businesses typically experience is chronic cash shortage. What comes in goes out almost immediately, and there's nothing left over! So, if something unexpected happens either personally or within the company that requires cash quickly, there's usually an insufficient amount of it on hand to take care of the problem. Also, there are other cash needs that a small business has that go unfunded for decades because all the cash is used up in the ongoing operation.

There are three main reasons why this happens:

1. Failure to identify and include cash reserves in the company's cash flow budget.

2. Failure to assign a high priority to the need for funding identified cash reserves.

3. A tendency for owners to become comfortable with their operating expense performance once all the bills are being regularly paid instead of constantly looking for ways to reduce operating expenses and improve efficiency.

A Reserve by definition is a particular cash account that has been separated out of normal operating cash and designated for a particular need in the future. The safe way to manage reserves is to set the reserved cash funds aside in a bank account fully separate from the account that handles normal operating cash. By doing that the reserved cash is not so easy to get to when an emergency arises and the owner might be tempted to dip into reserves instead of meeting the problem with ongoing cash generation.

The essence of the three reasons for never-funded reserve needs is that they're typically overlooked or procrastinated on by the small business owner. But the way it should work is that once a need for reserved funds is identified, it should be assigned a high enough priority so that the related funds will flow to it monthly from operating revenue instead of as an afterthought out of the rare occasions when cash is left over at the end of the period after all the other bills have been paid. Some people even pay some operating cost bills early instead of funding the reserves which at the least ought to be looked at on the same level of priority as the other bills.

Following now are four major kinds of Cash Reserves that should carry a high priority in your small business:

Payroll Tax Fund

If you have employees, you'll be collecting payroll taxes from your employees on behalf of the state and federal governments. Those funds are no longer yours the moment you deduct them from your employees' paychecks. They belong to the taxing authority and you are now a trustee for those funds until you have turned them over to the government along with the required accounting and paperwork. Payroll Tax monies should ALWAYS be set aside into a separate bank account so they aren't comingled with your operating cash. Over the years I have seen a number of small business owners get confused and use payroll tax funds for operating cash needs so that the cash isn't available when it comes time to pay the state.

DO NO DO THIS! Be a good steward of the government's funds and in doing that you'll learn how to treat the other reserves that you set up. In other words, if the small business owner would faithfully move the cash over from the operating account into the other reserve accounts and then treat the reserve money as if it belongs to somebody else, then the chance of bringing the funds back into the operating side of the business will be minimized.

Contingency Fund

One of the most typical signs of under-capitalization in small business is the inability to pay immediate cash for unexpected emergencies. When those things happen, and believe me they WILL happen, the company with no cash has to pay for it with additional, involuntary indebtedness. That debt will then have to be repaid in the future from revenue that's already committed to the ongoing operating needs of the company. The additional debt payments put a strain on the operation and make the cash shortage even greater. If you have enough unanticipated emergencies with no cash to pay for them, you'll eventually go out of business!

Many financial pundits recommend that small businesses need to work up to a Contingency Reserve of 3 to 6 months of average operating costs.[16] There are other factors involved in deriving the optimum amount for a particular business but this is a reasonable target for the typical scenario.

One thing to be clear about before moving on is that this Reserve Fund is for the contingency needs of the company, not for personal needs. The family also needs to have a contingency in their personal budget and we recommend an amount between $2,500 as an initial level up to about 6 months of gross income. Gross income is the amount of salary the owner receives from the small business BEFORE any deductions.

Savings Fund

When you get into small business ownership and it has become your main source of income, you'll want to arrange to SAVE some of your profits. If you worked for somebody in the past then they might have provided some sort of matching savings plan as part of a benefits package where you were able to put some of your money into a savings plan and it was "matched" at some level by

---

[16] https://www.score.org/blog/how-much-cash-should-small-business-keep-reserve

your employer. Now that you're working for your own company, you'll need to try to reproduce that same kind of plan: you put a part of your salary into a savings account that your company provides and the company matches that with a similar contribution. You'll want to confer with a CPA and Estate Planner to be sure that you set this program up so that you enjoy the optimum effect on your overall tax situation.

Among other things you will need to become familiar with the guidelines for IRA deductions. IRA stands for *Individual Retirement Accounts* and taxpayers are allowed to deduct a portion of their taxable income and deposit it into a formal retirement savings account. The formulas for dealing with IRA's are beyond the scope of this publication and are subject to change. Also, there are two different kinds of IRA's, tax deferred and tax paid which will figure into your future retirement plans. So, you should consult with your CPA to determine how much you can deduct from your income to help stimulate your retirement savings as advantageously as possible.

One of the potential problems that small business owners get into is that they PROCRASTINATE on setting aside savings. In the beginning of the business venture, cash flow is tight and the business owner is focusing on getting all the current bills paid and on using available capital to expand the business. Before you know it, twenty years have passed by and still no savings plan. Now everything is going to cost more and the reality is, if you ever expect to retire to some less active level in the future after age 65, you'll not be able to come close to continuing your standard of living at a similar level that you've been enjoying unless you have savings that have been invested and have grown sufficiently to provide you with continuing income for life. The big questions that need to be asked and answered by the entrepreneur as early as possible are these:

1. What age do I want to assume as a retirement target? Most entrepreneurs retire later in life but at some point we all have to slow down.

2. How much income will I need at that time to continue living at the same or a higher standard of living? Most people assume they will spend less after retirement on living expenses but actually the opposite is more likely because of additional traveling expenses. And don't forget to include the expected negative effects on the value of the dollar caused by inflation.

3. Based on the amount of income I want to receive after retiring, how much of an estate do I need to accumulate by my retirement date?

4. How is that accumulated savings going to be distributed back to my family and me and what happens if I live a lot longer than the actuarial forecast?

5. How will my spouse and family be cared for if I should die younger than the actuarial forecast?

There are two kinds of professionals you'll need to consult with to develop intelligent answers to these questions: the first is your CPA and the second is your Insurance/Estate Planning professional. You'll need the CPA to be sure you set up the accounting correctly and you'll need the estate planner to help you answer these five key questions.

The basic idea is that your Savings Fund should consist of two parts: the conservative, low-risk part and the investment-growth part. The younger you are when you start your fund, the more aggressive you can be, reaching for higher rates of growth with higher risk investments. But there should always be the two parts and few people are that organized because they usually put all their savings into high risk growth funds when they're starting. Then when they get older they're still heavily invested in high risk funds until they retire and suddenly put everything into CD's that have the lowest return on investment there is other than putting all your savings under your mattress.

A healthy estate needs to be built up with the following major components:

- Cash
- Real Estate
- Securities Investments
- Life Insurance
- Safe Insurance Annuities you cannot outlive

- Disability Insurance
- Tax Protection including trusts, family ownership, etc.
- The value of your small business
- Etc. as recommended by your Estate Planner

The purpose of this publication is to simply point out that you need to consider these things and not procrastinate until you're almost ready to retire and you're trying to figure out something to make up for lost time. When you are first starting your business, develop a budget form that fits your operation and INCLUDE these Reserve Funds in the form even though at the beginning you may not have enough cash flow to fund them. Put them in the form anyway so you don't forget them and one day you WILL be able to fund those reserves with a high priority.

Self-Funded Medical Insurance

If your company grows because of all your preparation and smart management, there may come a day when it would be in the cash flow interests of your company to consider self-funding your employee medical insurance. This isn't the appropriate publication to go into very much detail about this subject but it's something to make a mental note of for the future. You will need to have a fund set up for this purpose and you'll arrange with an appropriate administration company to handle the claims for your company. For many small businesses this will be a way to increase cash flow.

Special Projects Fund

From time-to-time you will see a future need for your company to spend funds for a special project. It could be new equipment or an office expansion or any of a number of needs that are large enough that they can't be paid for in cash out of the current operation. Rather than move ahead with the project by going into debt, you could consider setting aside cash for the project each month until the necessary amount has been accumulated in Reserve and you can proceed with a cash purchase. The key to it is that once the need has been identified you are disciplined enough to continue setting aside the funds on a regular basis until the target amount has been accumulated. Not everything the small business needs has to necessarily generate related indebtedness and not everything has to be purchased immediately. Why not wait a while if you can to avoid the additional debt and the related strain on your cash flow.

In concluding this chapter, the main takeaway is that successful business requires discipline combined with administrative and financial knowledge. You don't have to know all the details but you DO need to know enough about these issues to call in professionals and experts in those fields that can provide you with good counsel that will make you and your company more successful.

FORCE your company to have enough cash on hand by using that discipline and by not procrastinating. Start early and keep it going!

Thanks be to God who gives us the victory through our Lord Jesus Christ.
 1 Corinthians 15:57

Thanks be to God who always leads us in triumph in Christ.
 2 Corinthians 2:14

I can do all things through Him who strengthens me.
 Philippians 4:13

12. Importance of Giving Your Business to God

The way I think about things, the most important advice I can give someone about being in business for oneself is that in order to have a successful venture, you should make Jesus your CEO. However, if you're not interested in a relationship with Him at this time, please feel free to skip this chapter because I would prefer not to pressure anyone. You can always come back to it later if you change your mind. God leaves it to each person to make his/her own decisions about the subject of relationship. Some folks want to have one and many don't and there are plenty of small business owners, in fact most of them, who don't pursue the relationship this chapter is talking about.

But if you DO want to know more, let's continue. In the long run you will not be able to have real success in things if you try to do everything yourself and take all the burdens home with you every night. And there WILL be burdens because all the challenges that come up will be yours instead of some big corporate employer like you used to work for. Indeed, being in business for yourself can be a blessing or a curse depending upon your mindset when you go into it.

When most people talk about being a success in business they're usually just talking about the financial part of it. The thought is you're a success if you make a lot of money. But finance is only part of it. You can be a big success financially and a bust emotionally. You can be making a lot of money and at the same time be under a huge amount of stress to the point of affecting your health. You can be financially well off but worried all the time about how you're going to keep it, or anxious about what would happen to you if you lost everything or afraid that some competitor is going to come around and take away everything you have.

But you can make Jesus your CEO and decide from the outset that you're not going to allow yourself to be subjected to all the pressure. And as you're approaching the end of this publication, if you don't know Jesus yet you can meet Him if you want to so you can start working together. The good news is that there's help waiting for anyone who will receive it by faith. All you have to do is ask for help, believe that you receive it and then speak out to others that you believe (Romans 10:9).

So, if you have never invited Jesus to become the Lord of your life, you can do so today by saying the following simple prayer:

Jesus I believe in you and I believe that you were resurrected from the grave so that I can be born again and receive eternal life. Therefore, I receive you today as my Lord and Savior and I thank you for forgiving my sins.

If you were sincere as you prayed this prayer, God has already come into your life and you are a new creation.

Congratulations! Now ask the Lord to lead you to a good bible teaching church where you can be developed to fulfill your potential in the Kingdom of God. And please send us an e-mail advising your decision so we can rejoice for you in our prayers. If you're unable to find a church, give us a call and we'll help you find a good one.

Now you are ready to make Jesus your CEO. When you have to make a decision, ask the Holy Spirit what you should do and then step out in Faith and do what you hear Him say. If you're presented with a problem or a burden don't carry it around yourself, give it to Jesus. You're not equipped to carry burdens around but He is and He wants to do all your heavy lifting for you.

And lastly, always seek first the Kingdom of God with your business. Put the Kingdom of God as your first priority ahead of your business and you won't go wrong. In fact, you can't go wrong. Do what you do for the Kingdom of God and success will follow you everywhere. It's all about the Kingdom and it's all about Jesus. Find out how to fit into that scenario and you will never regret going into business for yourself.

GET SET GO !

13. Some Final Thoughts

The purpose of this publication is to INTRODUCE you to a complicated subject. Whole libraries have been written on the same ideas as this book. Our approach has been to summarize the highlights that you can use on a practical level to accomplish two purposes:

1. To make it possible for you to start a home-based business in a way and with enough knowledge to prepare you for both present tax optimization and future financial success.

2. To provide additional information beyond the startup phase to prepare you for the future as your home business matures and succeeds.

In addition to what you've been exposed to in this book, it's a good idea to talk to other people you respect and most importantly talk to people who have demonstrated entrepreneurial SUCCESS in their past so you can be advised from experience instead of opinion. Spend some time doing research to learn what it takes to be a successful entrepreneur. Buy some books on the subject and study to be informed. Avoid the temptation to step out impatiently, impetuously and unprepared.

At the beginning of this book we mentioned that if your carefully reviewed everything in this book and have a reasonable understanding of the material, there is a demonstrated probability that you will be successful. There is a process to go through:

1. You go ahead and set up a home-based business with the immediate objective of tax optimization.
2. You follow the 10-step startup plan presented in Chapter 5 in preparation for introducing the sale of products and/or services through your new company once you are ready.
3. You study available material particularly in the business financial area as you prepare for future growth and financial success.

> WE PARTICULARLY RECOMMEND OUR ADVANCED BOOK ON THIS SUBJECT:
>
> *Employee to Employer in 90 Days*
>
> PURCHASE THIS BOOK ON AMAZON.COM AT "Dr. Bill Miller" or through THE FOLLOWING LINK:
>
> https://www.amazon.com/Employee-EmployerDays-BillMiller/dp/1518622410/ref=sr_1_14?ie=UTF8&qid=1510245848&sr=8-14&keywords=Dr.+Bill+Miller

We are hopeful that in due course an increasing number of people will want to move out of big corporations, where they have become dependent on a secular materialistic system, to oversee their own business. The chance for full success in business and in life is dramatically increased if you consult God as you go along, if you don't get in a hurry and if you prepare adequately for what you're about to do.

If you need help with questions that develop as you're preparing to go into business for yourself, please feel free to call us toll free at any time: (800) 357-4223. There is no charge just for talking things over: just mention that you have acquired this book and have some questions that weren't answered in it. We'll be happy to talk to you because no one can publish a complete publication on such a complicated subject. It's entirely predictable that you may come up with some issues that weren't anticipated.

About Make A Way Ministries

For your information, *Make A Way Ministries Publications* is the publisher of this book and is a 501 C-3 non-profit corporation. The Ministry is fully able to provide efficient service to consumers anywhere in the US. You can reach them as follows:

>Make A Way Ministries
>P.O. Box 1164
>Granbury, Texas 76048
>
>Local: (817) 533-9499
>Local: (305) 271-5094
>Toll Free: (800) 357-4223

Fax: (305) 271-1826

Email: cfc@creditcounseling.net
Web Site: www.creditcounseling.net

Make A Way Ministries has been providing credit and financial counseling and teaching across the U.S. since 1987. All financial publications are based on biblical principles and great care is taken to provide information that truly benefits our clients. We would never recommend a publication just to take your money. We pray that God will bless your efforts and reward you with His promised prosperity in accordance with His will for your life.

Donations

If you would like to make a donation to help cover the operating costs of the ministry, please make your offering payable to *Make A Way Ministries* and send it to the address shown above. Even better you can also text your donation to 817-592-9003 OR go to the following link: *https://app.clovergive.com/g3/*

By the Word of God we're certain that He will multiply your donation back to you. Gifts to *Make A Way Ministries* are normally tax deductible. May God bless you with His abundant harvest in return for sowing your precious seed into this Ministry!

APPENDIX ONE:

How to Apply for an SBA Loan

Introduction

As you now know, most small businesses fail during their first five years of life. The tragic statistic is that 75% of them WILL fail based on past experience. The reason they will fail is that the owners don't possess enough business knowledge when they start their businesses and those businesses tend to be undercapitalized.

There's nothing that can replace business knowledge and get success instead of failure. No business knowledge = no success. That's the equation that almost ALWAYS confirms itself even though millions of people continue trying to prove it wrong.

Under capitalization is another matter. In fact, the federal government has set up an operation called the *Small Business Administration (SBA)* that specializes in making available training and capital to small business people to help them succeed instead of fail. If you conclude that your business can support some amount of indebtedness in order to have sufficient capitalization available, the SBA may be a good place to look.

The way it works is that the SBA guarantees loans through the banks of your choice assuming you meet all of the requirements. Some banks specialize in handling these kinds of loans and it's probably smart to look for one and they will usually have a Loan Officer on their team that is particularly knowledgeable.

In the remainder of this Appendix you will find a series of articles that will help you prepare for the pursuit of an SBA loan. Be prepared for a process with a lot of details but hopefully at the end you will find the optimum capitalization for your small business.

Loan Application Checklist

Once you have decided to apply for a loan guaranteed by the SBA, you will need to collect the appropriate documents for your application. The SBA does not provide direct loans. The process starts with your local lender, working within SBA guidelines.

Use the checklist below to ensure you have everything the lender will ask for to complete your application. Once your loan package is complete, your lender will submit it to the SBA.

1. **SBA Loan Application** – To begin the process, you will need to complete an SBA loan application form at the following URL:

    - Borrower Information Form – SBA Form 1919
      https://www.sba.gov/sites/default/files/SBA%20Form%201919%204-28-14_review.pdf

2. **Personal Background and Financial Statement** – To assess your eligibility, the SBA also requires you to complete the following forms that can be accessed on-line at the indicated URL addresses:

    - *Statement of Personal History* - SBA Form 912

      https://www.sba.gov/sites/default/files/forms/SBA%20%20Form%20912%20%202-13.pdf

    - *Personal Financial Statement* - SBA Form 413

      https://www.sba.gov/sites/default/files/forms/SBA_Form_413_7a-504-SBG.pdf

3. **Business Financial Statements** – To support your application and demonstrate your ability to repay the loan, prepare and include the following financial statements:

    - *Profit and Loss (P&L) Statement* – This must be current within 180 days of your application. Also include supplementary schedules from the last three fiscal years.

    - *Projected Financial Statements* – Include a detailed, one-year projection of income and finances and attach a written explanation as to how you expect to achieve this projection.

4. **Ownership and Affiliations** – Include a list of names and addresses of any subsidiaries and affiliates, including concerns in which you hold a controlling interest and other concerns that may be affiliated by stock ownership, franchise, proposed merger or otherwise with you.

5. **Business Certificate/License** – Your original business license or certificate of doing business. If your business is a corporation, stamp your corporate seal on the SBA loan application form.

6. **Loan Application History** – Include records of any loans you may have applied for in the past.

7. **Income Tax Returns** – Include signed *personal* and *business* federal income tax returns of your business' principals for previous three years.

8. **Résumés** – Include personal résumés for each principal.

9. **Business Overview and History** – Provide a brief history of the business and its challenges. Include an explanation of why the SBA loan is needed and how it will help the business.

10. **Business Lease** – Include a copy of your business lease, or note from your landlord, giving terms of proposed lease.

11. **If You are Purchasing an Existing Business** – The following information is needed for purchasing an existing business:

    - Current balance sheet and P&L statement of business to be purchased
    - Previous two years federal income tax returns of the business
    - Proposed Bill of Sale including Terms of Sale
    - Asking price with schedule of inventory, machinery and equipment, furniture and fixtures

5 Tips for Successfully Navigating the SBA Loan Application Process

By Caron_Beesley, SBA Contributor
Published: February 19, 2013
Updated: September 3, 2015

In the market for a business loan? Heard about SBA loans but not really sure how they work or how to go about applying for one?

The following are common questions that small business owners have about SBA loan programs and the loan application process.

1. How do SBA loans work?

While the SBA does offer numerous loan programs to help small business owners finance their businesses, it doesn't actually lend businesses the money. Instead, a bank makes the loan, which is backed by the SBA. This allows the bank to take a little more risk than they otherwise might.

So this means that if you are seeking a business loan and don't qualify for a traditional bank loan, perhaps because you don't have the collateral or years in business to justify the loan, the government can help – although you still need to work primarily with a bank.

2. Who makes the decision that an SBA loan is right for my business?

If you've been turned down for a traditional bank loan, or are curious about SBA loan programs, where should you start? Should you go to the bank and ask for an SBA loan, or would they instinctively guide you towards one? While your local SBA district office can help explain the available loan programs and determine your eligibility for them, you'll need to find a local SBA lender to kick-start the application process. These banks and financial institutions can help you determine which loan program might be right for you, whether it's a traditional bank loan or an SBA-backed loan. They are also your point of contact for processing your loan application.

3. How do I determine which SBA loan is right for me?

The SBA offers numerous loan programs depending on your business profile, financing needs, growth plans and so on. There are a number of ways to identify the right loan program for your business.

If you are in the early stages of exploring your financing options, check out the SBA's Online Loans and Grants Search Tool. Answer a few quick questions about your business and the tool will suggest government financing programs for which you might qualify.

Once you've done your research, consult your local SBA District Office and ask them to steer you towards a few SBA lenders in your area so that you can be sure you're getting the right loan program for your business – and the right bank!

4. How should I prepare for my meeting with the bank?

Preparation is key and it's important to understand some of the criteria that might influence your eligibility for an

SBA loan. These include credit factors – such as making timely debt payments (payment on existing credit relationships, both business and personal, is considered an indicator of your ability to repay a loan), cash flow projections and your debt-to-worth ratio. Collateral and working capital are other factors that may impact eligibility.

SBA offers guidance on all the factors that lenders look at <u>here</u>.

You'll also need to ensure you are in good standing with your state treasury and the IRS (i.e., you've paid all taxes owed).

And don't forget the most important document – your business plan with at least three years of financial projections; a view of what you'll do with the proceeds of the loan; and solid proof that you know your industry and target market. This is particularly important for start-ups that don't have a financial history. The bank will base its decision on your industry experience and future plans.
If you don't have a business plan, check out SBA's <u>Build your Business Plan Tool</u> – a step-by-step guide to help you get started. You can save the plan as you go and download it when you're done.

5. What do I need to complete my SBA loan application?

An incomplete loan application won't do you any favors with the bank and could slow down the entire loan process. Familiarize yourself in advance with the key components of the loan application – from the right forms, to the necessary background information. Refer to this SBA Loan Application Checklist to ensure you have all your i's dotted and t's crossed. SBA also offers a free online training course: How to Prepare a Loan Package.

Business Loans – What Lenders Look for and Tips for Winning Them Over

By Caron_Beesley, SBA Contributor
Published: January 22, 2013
Updated: September 3, 2015

Securing small business financing can be challenging. Whether you are just starting out or looking to grow, banks and lending institutions can be rigorous in their lending review practices.

For example, businesses with few assets to their name may find it hard to secure a traditional loan. Other business owners may not be able to provide the reassurance that lenders seek to alleviate their concerns that your business may fail and the loan won't get repaid. So when you approach a lender, it's just as important to understand the basis on which loans are made as it is to stack up your financials and business plan.

So what are lenders looking for in a potential loan applicant? Here's what you need to know.

Loan Applicants Need to Check off Several Boxes

What are loan officers looking for when approached about a loan? Here are some basic "must-haves" that the ideal candidate might be expected to evidence:

- That you have sufficient assets, financial reserves and personal collateral to endure business fluctuations (and still pay off your loan).

- As an existing business owner, you'll need to show that you have solid cash flow, sufficient to repay the loan.

- New businesses need to evidence that they have a track record of profitability and success in a similar business endeavor.

Let's face it, that's a tricky list for any prospective or existing small business! So what are your options? Proving your creditworthiness is still possible, with some planning and preparation.

How to Prove Your Creditworthiness

Bankers need to make money, and while they may have an ideal candidate in mind, even they have to compromise—this is where your opportunity lies. The trick is to demonstrate, using other means, that you are a creditworthy business owner. For example, if you are new to this business, can you show success in managing a similar business another field (even if you weren't the owner)? Perhaps you've owned or managed a profitable business in a different industry? Lending officers might be more agreeable to your application if you can show that you supplement your own experience with that of someone who also has success in the field.

Putting yourself in the lender's shoes is a good starting point. It's much like a job interview, where you form an understanding of the type of candidate the employer is looking for and prepare your application and anticipate questions accordingly. Ask yourself: "Why should this lender think my business can succeed where others have failed?" and have a thorough answer prepared, plus a detailed explanation of how the money will be used and your plan for paying it off.

Step Back and Prepare

Key to this preparation is a solid business plan, good personal and business credit, and some expert help. The following SBA resources and tools can help guide you down this preparation path:

- **Build a Business Plan Online Tool** – Putting pen to paper to write a business plan isn't the easiest of tasks. Check out this new tool from SBA that guides small business owners through the process of creating a basic, downloadable business plan—and offers pointers on essential elements like cash flow and financial projections. The great thing about this tool is you can build a plan in smaller bites, save your progress and return at your leisure.

- **Clean Up Your Credit** – Business credit is an asset and considered an economic resource that makes up the financial foundation of a company. Lenders look for assets. SBA guest blogger Marco Carbajo blogs regularly about how to build your business and personal credit to help secure financing. Check out his article: *How To Build Business Credit For Your Start Up*, and view more of Marco's articles here on the SBA website.

- **Consult an Expert** – Whether you need help finding the right loan for your business or a guiding hand that can help you through the application process, don't feel that you have to go it alone. Local Small Business Development Centers, Women's Business

Centers, and SCORE (a mentoring organization for small businesses) can help you through the process. Find one of these groups in your community.

Can't Get a Business Loan? Consider Alternative Financing from SBA Loan Programs

If you or your lender decides that you aren't the right candidate for a traditional business loan, you still have options. Consider an SBA Loan Program. The SBA doesn't lend businesses money; instead, these programs take the risk away from the banks and encourage them to make loans to small business owners by guaranteeing part of the loan.

Check out these additional online learning resources that can help you navigate the SBA loan process:

APPENDIX TWO
Financial Statements for Beginners

Financial Statements for Beginners

The Basics

If you can read a nutrition label or a baseball box score, you can learn to read basic financial statements. If you can follow a recipe or apply for a loan, you can learn basic accounting. The basics aren't difficult and they aren't rocket science.

This brochure is designed to help you gain a basic understanding of how to read financial statements. Just as a CPR class teaches you how to perform the basics of cardiac pulmonary resuscitation, this brochure will explain how to read the basic parts of a financial statement. It will not train you to be an accountant (just as a CPR course will not make you a cardiac doctor), but it should give you the confidence to be able to look at a set of financial statements and make sense of them.
Let's begin by looking at what financial statements do.

"Show me the money!"

We all remember Cuba Gooding Jr.'s immortal line from the movie *Jerry Maguire*, "Show me the money!" Well, that's what financial statements do. They show you the money. They show you where a company's money came from, where it went, and where it is now.

There are four main financial statements. They are: (1) balance sheets; (2) income statements; (3) cash flow statements; and (4) statements of shareholders' equity. Balance sheets show what a company owns and what it owes at a fixed point in time. Income statements show how much money a company made and spent over a period of time. Cash flow statements show the exchange of money between a company and the outside world also over a period of time. The fourth financial statement, called a "statement of shareholders' equity," shows changes in the interests of the company's shareholders over time.

Let's look at each of the first three financial statements in more detail.

Balance Sheets

A balance sheet provides detailed information about a company's assets, liabilities and shareholders' equity.

Assets are things that a company owns that have value. This typically means they can either be sold or used by the company to make products or provide services that can be sold. Assets include physical property, such as plants, trucks, equipment and inventory. It also includes things that can't be touched but nevertheless exist and have value, such as trademarks and patents. And cash itself is an asset. So are investments a company makes.

Liabilities are amounts of money that a company owes to others. This can include all kinds of obligations, like money borrowed from a bank to launch a new product, rent for use of a building, money owed to suppliers for materials, payroll a company owes to its employees, environmental cleanup costs, or taxes owed to the government. Liabilities also include obligations to provide goods or services to customers in the future.

Shareholders' equity is sometimes called capital or net worth. It's the money that would be left if a company sold all of its assets and paid off all of its liabilities. This leftover money belongs to the shareholders, or the owners, of the company.

> The following formula summarizes what a balance sheet shows:
>
> ASSETS = LIABILITIES + NET WORTH
>
> A company's assets have to equal, or "balance," the sum of its liabilities and shareholders' equity.

A company's balance sheet is set up like the basic accounting equation shown above. On the left side of the balance sheet, companies list their assets. On the right side, they list their liabilities and shareholders' equity. Sometimes balance sheets show assets at the top, followed by liabilities, with shareholders' equity at the bottom.

Assets are generally listed based on how quickly they will be converted into cash. <u>Current</u> assets are things a company expects to convert to cash within one year. A good example is inventory. Most companies expect to sell their inventory for cash within one year. <u>Noncurrent</u> assets are things a company does not expect to convert to cash within one year or that would take longer than one year to sell. Noncurrent assets include <u>fixed</u> assets. <u>Fixed</u> assets are those assets used to operate the business but that are not available for sale, such as trucks, office furniture and other property.

Liabilities are generally listed based on their due dates. Liabilities are said to be either <u>current</u> or <u>long-term</u>. <u>Current</u> liabilities are obligations a company expects to pay off within the year. <u>Long-term</u> liabilities are obligations due more than one year away.

Shareholders' equity is the amount owners invested in the company's stock plus or minus the company's earnings or losses since inception. Sometimes companies distribute earnings, instead of retaining them. These distributions are called dividends.

A balance sheet shows a snapshot of a company's assets, liabilities and shareholders' equity at the end of the reporting period. It does not show the flows into and out of the accounts during the period.

Income Statements

An income statement is a report that shows how much revenue a company earned over a specific time period (usually for a year or some portion of a year). An income statement also shows the costs and expenses associated with earning that revenue. The literal "bottom line" of the statement usually shows the company's net earnings or losses. This tells you how much the company earned or lost over the period.

Income statements also report earnings per share (or "EPS"). This calculation tells you how much money shareholders would receive if the company decided to distribute all of the net earnings for the period. (Companies almost never distribute all of their earnings. Usually they reinvest them in the business.)

To understand how income statements are set up, think of them as a set of stairs. You start at the top with the total amount of sales made during the accounting period. Then you go down, one step at a time. At each step, you make a deduction for certain costs or other operating expenses associated with earning the revenue. At the bottom of the stairs, after deducting all of the expenses, you learn how much the company actually earned or lost during the accounting period. People often call this "the bottom line."

At the top of the income statement is the total amount of money brought in from sales of products or services. This top line is often referred to as gross revenues or sales. It's called "gross" because expenses have not been deducted from it yet. So the number is "gross" or unrefined.

The next line is money the company doesn't expect to collect on certain sales. This could be due, for example, to sales discounts or merchandise returns.

When you subtract the returns and allowances from the gross revenues, you arrive at the company's net revenues. It's called "net" because, if you can imagine a net, these revenues are left in the net after the deductions for returns and allowances have come out.

Moving down the stairs from the net revenue line, there are several lines that represent various kinds of operating expenses. Although these lines can be reported in various orders, the next line after net revenues typically shows the costs of the sales. This number tells you the amount of money the company spent to produce the goods or services it sold during the accounting period.

The next line subtracts the costs of sales from the net revenues to arrive at a subtotal called "gross profit" or sometimes "gross margin."

It's considered "gross" because there are certain expenses that haven't been deducted from it yet.

The next section deals with operating expenses. These are expenses that go toward supporting a company's operations for a given period – for example, salaries of administrative personnel and costs of researching new products. Marketing expenses are another example. Operating expenses are different from "costs of sales," which were deducted above, because operating expenses cannot be linked directly to the production of the products or services being sold.

Depreciation is also deducted from gross profit. Depreciation takes into account the wear and tear on some assets, such as machinery, tools and furniture, which are used over the long term. Companies spread the cost of these assets over the periods they are used. This process of spreading these costs is called depreciation or amortization. The "charge" for using these assets during the period is a fraction of the original cost of the assets.

After all operating expenses are deducted from gross profit, you arrive at operating profit before interest and income tax expenses. This is often called "income from operations."

Next companies must account for interest income and interest expense. Interest income is the money companies make from keeping their cash in interest-bearing savings accounts, money market funds and the like. On the other hand, interest expense is the money companies paid in interest for money they borrow. Some income statements show interest income and interest expense separately. Some income statements combine the two numbers. The interest income and expense are then added or subtracted from the operating profits to arrive at operating profit <u>before</u> income tax.

Finally, income tax is deducted and you arrive at the bottom line: net profit or net losses. (Net profit is also called net income or net earnings.) This tells you how much the company actually earned or lost during the accounting period. Did the company make a profit or did it lose money?

Earnings Per Share or EPS
Most income statements include a calculation of earnings per share or EPS. This calculation tells you how much money shareholders would receive for each share of stock they own if the company distributed all of its net income for the period.

To calculate EPS, you take the total net income and divide it by the number of outstanding shares of the company.

Cash Flow Statements
Cash flow statements report a company's inflows and outflows of cash. This is important because a company needs to have enough cash on hand to pay its expenses and purchase assets. While an income statement can tell you whether a company made a profit, a cash flow statement can tell you whether the company generated cash.

A cash flow statement shows changes over time rather than absolute dollar amounts at a point in time. It uses and reorders the information from a company's balance sheet and income statement.

The bottom line of the cash flow statement shows the net increase or decrease in cash for the period. Generally, cash flow statements are divided into three main parts. Each part reviews the cash flow from one of three types of activities: (1) operating activities; (2) investing activities; and (3) financing activities.

Operating Activities
The first part of a cash flow statement analyzes a company's cash flow from net income or losses. For most companies, this section of the cash flow statement reconciles the net income (as shown on the income statement) to the actual cash the company received from or used in its operating activities. To do this, it adjusts net income for any non-cash items (such as adding back depreciation expenses) and adjusts for any cash that was used or provided by other operating assets and liabilities.

Investing Activities
The second part of a cash flow statement shows the cash flow from all investing activities, which generally include purchases or sales of

long-term assets, such as property, plant and equipment, as well as investment securities. If a company buys a piece of machinery, the cash flow statement would reflect this activity as a cash outflow from investing activities because it used cash. If the company decided to sell off some investments from an investment portfolio, the proceeds from the sales would show up as a cash inflow from investing activities because it provided cash.

Financing Activities
The third part of a cash flow statement shows the cash flow from all financing activities. Typical sources of cash flow include cash raised by selling stocks and bonds or borrowing from banks. Likewise, paying back a bank loan would show up as a use of cash flow.

Read the Footnotes

A horse called "Read The Footnotes" ran in the 2004 Kentucky Derby. He finished seventh, but if he had won, it would have been a victory for financial literacy proponents everywhere. It's so important to *read the footnotes*. The footnotes to financial statements are packed with information. Here are some of the highlights:

- Significant accounting policies and practices – Companies are required to disclose the accounting policies that are most important to the portrayal of the company's financial condition and results. These often require management's most difficult, subjective or complex judgments.

- Income taxes – The footnotes provide detailed information about the company's current and deferred income taxes. The information is broken down by level – federal, state, local and/or foreign, and the main items that affect the company's effective tax rate are described.

- Pension plans and other retirement programs – The footnotes discuss the company's pension plans and other retirement or post-employment benefit programs. The notes contain specific information about the assets and costs of these programs, and indicate whether and by how much the plans are over- or under-funded.

- Stock options – The notes also contain information about stock options granted to officers and employees, including the method of accounting for stock-based compensation and the effect of the method on reported results.

Read the MD&A

You can find a narrative explanation of a company's financial performance in a section of the quarterly or annual report entitled, "Management's Discussion and Analysis of Financial Condition and Results of Operations." MD&A is *management's* opportunity to provide investors with its view of the financial performance and condition of the company. It's management's opportunity to tell investors what the financial statements show and do not show, as well as important trends and risks that have shaped the past or are reasonably likely to shape the company's future.

The SEC's rules governing MD&A require disclosure about trends, events or uncertainties known to management that would have a material impact on reported financial information. The purpose of MD&A is to provide investors with information that the company's management believes to be necessary to an understanding of its financial condition, changes in financial condition and results of operations. It is intended to help investors to see the company through the eyes of management. It is also intended to provide context for the financial statements and information about the company's earnings and cash flows.

Financial Statement Ratios and Calculations

You've probably heard people banter around phrases like "P/E ratio," "current ratio" and "operating margin." But what do these terms mean and why don't they show up on financial statements? Listed below are just some of the many ratios that investors calculate from information on financial statements and then use to evaluate a company. As a general rule, desirable ratios vary by industry.

If a company has a debt-to-equity ratio of 2 to 1, it means that the company has two dollars of debt to every one dollar shareholders invest in the company. In other words, the company is taking on debt at twice the rate that its owners are investing in the company.

Inventory Turnover Ratio = Cost of Sales / Average Inventory for the Period

If a company has an inventory turnover ratio of 2 to 1, it means that the company's inventory turned over twice in the reporting period.

Operating Margin = Income from Operations / Net Revenues

Operating margin is usually expressed as a percentage. It shows, for each dollar of sales, what percentage was profit.

P/E Ratio = Price per share / Earnings per share

If a company's stock is selling at $20 per share and the company is earning $2 per share, then the company's P/E Ratio is 10 to 1. The company's stock is selling at 10 times its earnings.

Working Capital = Current Assets – Current Liabilities
- *Debt-to-equity ratio* compares a company's total debt to shareholders' equity. Both of these numbers can be found on a company's balance sheet. To calculate debt-to-equity ratio, you divide a company's total liabilities by its shareholder equity, or
- *Inventory turnover ratio* compares a company's cost of sales on its income statement with its average inventory balance for the period. To calculate the average inventory balance for the period, look at the inventory numbers listed on the balance sheet. Take the balance listed for the period of the report and add it to the balance listed for the previous comparable period, and then divide by two. (Remember that balance sheets are snapshots in time. So the inventory balance for the previous period is the beginning balance for the current period, and the

inventory balance for the current period is the ending balance.) To calculate the inventory turnover ratio, you divide a company's cost of sales (just below the net revenues on the income statement) by the average inventory for the period, or
- *Operating margin* compares a company's operating income to net revenues. Both of these numbers can be found on a company's income statement. To calculate operating margin, you divide a company's income from operations (before interest and income tax expenses) by its net revenues, or
- *P/E ratio* compares a company's common stock price with its earnings per share. To calculate a company's P/E ratio, you divide a company's stock price by its earnings per share, or
- *Working capital* is the money leftover if a company paid its current liabilities (that is, its debts due within one-year of the date of the balance sheet) from its current assets.

Bringing It All Together

Although this brochure discusses each financial statement separately, keep in mind that they are all related. The changes in assets and liabilities that you see on the balance sheet are also reflected in the revenues and expenses that you see on the income statement, which result in the company's gains or losses. Cash flows provide more information about cash assets listed on a balance sheet and are related, but not equivalent, to net income shown on the income statement. And so on. No one financial statement tells the complete story. But combined, they provide very powerful information for investors. And information is the investor's best tool when it comes to investing wisely.

Source: U.S. Securities and Exchange Commission, February 5, 2007
"Beginners' Guide to Financial Statements"

https://www.sec.gov/reportspubs/investorpublications/investorpubsbegfinstmtguidehtm.html

APPENDIX THREE:

Eight Basic Secrets of Financial Success

The following article was written a number of years ago and talks about the eight major things in life that produce financial success. Everyone who starts a business needs to be mindful of these principles and if you are, it's way more likely that you will turn out to be a financial success.

EIGHT BASIC SECRETS OF FINANCIAL SUCCESS
(AKA: HOW TO HANDLE YOUR MONEY)

Almost everybody wants to be a financial success. Even the ones who believe they'll never be successful would like to be if they could just find a way. The problem is most people don't know the way; they don't know how to do it. They think it's about making more money. But most rich people didn't get to be rich because somebody paid them more money or because one day they finally won the lottery. No, they became rich because they had a plan to go somewhere, they pursued that plan day after day and they did a good job of HANDLING whatever money they had on hand along the way. And oh by the way, most so-called rich people are NOT financially successful either.

What does it mean then to be *financially successful?* If you were living in some third-world country you'd be *financially successful* if you had enough to eat, if you had fresh water to drink and if you had a roof over your head. But since you live in the USA where materialism is king, the standards for financial success are higher. We want to have a lot of possessions and our definition of success is reserved for people who have a lot of them including big houses, big cars, a lot of expensive clothes, etc. But did you know MOST of the people who go around showing off those kinds of things either owe some creditor for them or they acquired a lot of it illegally? They're usually tortured by fear that they could lose all their acquired stuff and that they could be left with nothing, stripped of all their assets and standing in Bankruptcy Court.

Friend, financial success is NOT about how much money and possessions you control. It's NOT about how much money you make. No, it's about the quality of your life that has resulted from how you've HANDLED the money that's come your way over the last 7 to 10 years of your life. And the measure of your success is how you feel about what you have: are you at peace with it all or do you live in fear, losing sleep or running from your creditors all the time? Is your credit rating so negative you're afraid to go and interview for a better job because you think no one will hire you? Are you embarrassed for someone to look at your credit reports?

A person who's *financially successful* is content, lives comfortably within his/her level of income, has all their essential needs met, has enough contingency funds set aside to deal with the emergencies of life, and has money left over to sow into the Kingdom of God and to bless family and other folks when those occasions arise. A person who's *financially successful* is someone who makes wise decisions with the long-range future in mind instead of just for the moment. A person who's *financial successful* is someone who lives by faith and trusts that God will take care of them. A person who's *financially successful* is not trying to get rich but the blessing of prosperity always finds them out anyway without having to strive for it.

In 1987 we started a credit counseling ministry here in Miami and over the years we've come in contact with tens of thousands of folks. As you'd expect almost all of them had some kind of credit problem. They came to us because they needed help in getting themselves out of some money situation that was holding them in bondage. So for a number of years now we've had a unique opportunity to come to some conclusions about what it takes to be *financially successful* and based on that experience we've been able to summarize the various qualities that produce SUCCESS down to eight of the basic PRACTICAL requirements that will ALWAYS produce good results. If you'll do these eight things it's virtually GUARANTEED that you WILL be a financial success in 7 years or less.

1. You Must Have a Family Budget and Live By It

   Most people don't have a budget. In fact, more than 85% of folks in the US have NEVER had a personal or family budget, wouldn't know how to put one together if they tried and think they don't need one. Nothing could be further from the truth. No operating entity from families to corporations that has money coming in and going out should try to make it all work without a budget. Lack of planning is one of the main reasons people are financially unsuccessful because they have no idea where the money they make is going.

Accompanying this article is a simple one-page Family Budget form that you can use to get organized. How do you spend your money? If you spend more than you bring in you'll either have to go broke or use indebtedness to make up the difference. *Financial success* comes from spending LESS than what you make, not more. And the way to be sure you'll always spend less is to write down ahead of time how you're going to spend your money. And then keep track of how you actually spent it compared to your plan. Most families live paycheck to paycheck and are essentially insolvent. Insolvency is when you owe more than you're worth. But in our experience we've only encountered a very few families who were budgeting before they came to see us because families who budget usually don't have financial problems. An essential requirement for *financial success* is to live by a budget. Nothing will work until you're willing to make this step.

A budget should be used as a guide to making your expenditures. It doesn't have to be some legal thing but at the end of the month you want to come out with totally expenditures that are less than your income. How you get to that objective every month is not as important as getting there. If during the month you see that you're going to overrun one of your budget categories then reassign the funds from one of the other budget categories where you can spend less than the budget. If you can come out at the end of the month CONSISTENTLY with your expenses less than your income you will be *financially successful* in no time.

2. You Must Avoid Indebtedness

We live in a society where almost everyone is in debt. It's part of our way of life and we don't think too much about it. If we want something we just take out a credit card or open a new charge account and more often than not we have only a vague idea of how we're going to pay back a new debt. The whole financial system in this country is based on the assumption that the consumer is willing to go into debt and pay their creditors outrageous amounts of interest for letting them borrow their money. And since consumers are willing to do it the banks and other creditors are eager to attract people who have relatively decent credit ratings and are willing to go into debt.

But here's a key point to know if you want to be *financially successful*: you can NEVER be *financial successful* and in debt at the same time. Indebtedness is the most formidable obstacle to success there is. It MUST be eliminated and then avoided like the plague because it's so toxic to success. Virtually 100% of all consumers who can be considered *financially successful* are DEBT FREE. The absolute <u>wrong</u> way to handle money is to go into debt to purchase possessions you think you can't wait for. To change that picture and have even a chance to be successful, you'll have to make a final no-compromise decision to stop using debt and then take action to make it happen to become DEBT FREE. No exceptions!

3. You Must ALWAYS Pay ALL Your Bills on Time

A lot of people are kind of blasé about paying their bills on time. They don't pay any attention to the official payment dates and just pay their bills when they get around to it. Other folks are trying to make their payments as late as possible just before the creditor cuts them off thinking they're winning some kind of dumb game. It's dumb because the system GREATLY favors the people who make all their payments on time and gives them the reputation as people of good character.

But did you know that every late payment you make is reported by your creditors as DEROGATORY information to the three national credit bureaus? And did you know that a pattern of late payments causes your FICO Scores to be significantly reduced? Lower scores means you pay higher interest. Lower scores mean you won't be seriously considered for the best jobs because employers interpret a history of late payments as an indication of a flawed character and irresponsibility. Lower scores mean your insurance costs will be higher. And most companies charge late fees which greatly increase the real cost of your credit.

So the correct way to handle your money is to be on top of your payments and pay them even before the due dates so you can be sure to not ever be late. Make it one of your highest priorities as it should be. Plan your payments for the times during the month when you receive your income and you know that you'll have the funds on hand. And don't forget that if you're mailing them you need to allow plenty of time for your checks to arrive at your creditors' offices. If they don't arrive on time they WILL be counted as late and you WILL have to pay late fees and you WILL be reported to the credit bureaus as having paid late. This is really, really important!

4. You Must Monitor Your Credit Reports

Most people have never seen their credit reports but if you have a social security number you definitely DO have credit reports. There're three national credit bureaus and each of them publishes a credit report that summarizes a lot of private information about every consumer in the country. Anyone that's specifically authorized by the law may review that private information about you by paying the appropriate fees to the credit bureaus. The publishing of private information is allowed by the law but credit bureaus are restricted as to how they may distribute the reports. Legally authorized users include prospective creditors, landlords, lenders, banks, insurance companies, prospective employers, etc.

Did you know that studies show that more than 70% of all credit reports contain errors or outdated information? Those errors could be costing you real money if they go on undetected because if they cause your FICO Scores to decrease, then your interest rates could go up. How're those errors detected? They'll be detected ONLY by concerned consumers who're regularly monitoring their credit reports. No one else will be looking for them. That means YOU have to be in charge of your own credit reports and insure that they are reflecting an accurate and as favorable picture of you as possible.

Another thing to be concerned about is that Identity Theft is the fastest growing white collar crime in the country. Most people find out about that they've been a victim of IT when they receive a bill or a call from a bill collector about a debt they never heard of before. But someone who is on top of their credit reports and is monitoring them every few months will catch a problem early in the process. Also, the smart consumer is probably going to have an alert service set up with the credit bureaus so the identity thieves will be unable to penetrate your defenses. The person who handles their money correctly is a person who PROTECTS their credit ratings and constantly monitors their credit reports.

You can obtain a FREE credit report annually from each of the three credit bureaus at:

www.annualcreditreport.com

We recommend down loading one at a time every four months during the year so that you're always working with recent information. You can also purchase one of the on-line monitoring services for about $15.00 per month. There're a number of good services and we particularly recommend the ones sold by the credit bureaus at the following web sites:

www.equifax.com
www.experian.com
www.transunion.com

5. You Must Stay Away From Get Rich Quick Schemes

There were three main reasons why so many families have had financial problems because of the recession: 1) reduced income, 2) indebtedness and 3) using debt to invest in real estate thinking they were going to get rich in a few months. Certainly reduced income has been hard to deal with. Unemployment and cutbacks are still at difficult levels. But the people who have had the most trouble are the ones who were in a significant amount of debt BEFORE the recession. Folks who didn't have any debt at all have been able to weather the storm much more effectively. But the ones who're the worse off are the people who were going into sub-prime mortgage debt they shouldn't have been able to qualify for trying to "flip" real estate and get rich QUICK.

Very few rich people ever got there QUICKLY. It almost NEVER happens that way. A basic principle of handling money is that the QUICKER something is the more RISKY it is. Leading up to every recession or depression or what they used to call "panics" in the history of our economy there has ALWAYS been a large group of people who were trying to pursue some scheme to get rick QUICK. They are SPECULATORS who push up prices to artificial levels only to eventually see the bursting of those price bubbles where they lose all their money.

The moral of the story is stay out of get rich QUICK schemes and speculations. Avoid them like the plague! They may sound good but if it's QUICK it's going to be RISKY and the person who's pursuing a course to *financial success* should be trying to avoid RISK as much as possible. Becoming *financially successful* is a slow, purposeful, step-by-step process of following a good plan of living within your budget, staying out of debt, putting money aside in conservative, low-risk investments that won't disappear when the next recession comes along and being content to wait to buy things until you have accumulated enough CASH.

6. You Must Avoid Co-signing

Now this next one is going to be hard because eventually some friend or family member with a bad credit rating is going to come to you with your good credit rating and ask you to CO-SIGN with them to help them go into debt. Most people these days give in to those requests because they want to be loved by their families and they want to love them back by helping them "progress" in life. But, you MUST resist the temptation if you want to be *financially successful.*

When you CO-SIGN with someone for a debt you are telling the creditor that if your loved one defaults on that debt YOU will pay it off on their behalf. You are GUARANTEEING that the debt will be paid. Do you have the money set aside for that possibility; otherwise if your loved one defaults you have just gone into debt. If the financial system found it too risky to give credit to your loved one, why would you want to take on the creditor's responsibility by taking the risk on your own shoulders? We have seem time after time the good financial ratings of otherwise debt free people ruined by having CO-SIGNED a debt they were not able to pay for when their loved one defaulted.

You will just have to resist the temptation to GUARANTEE someone's debt. Why would you want to help someone go into debt when your value for yourself is to stay out of debt? No, tough love is better for both sides in these situations. The better approach would be to gift your money to your loved one as you can afford it into a savings account <u>that you control</u> with both parties contributing into that account as you've agreed together until there's enough money accumulated there to pay CASH for the thing they had originally wanted you to CO-SIGN for. Debt is NEVER the right answer for someone who's working to be *financially successful* and the hard truth is that CO-SIGNING often leads to debt!

7. You Must Have a Contingency Fund

The purpose of a Contingency Fund is to have money set aside to be used ONLY in the case of emergencies. We're all going to experience emergencies from time to time that we had no way to plan for. For example, you need a new battery for your car (they cost more than $100 these days) or new tires or your washer or dryer goes out or there's a medical emergency you hadn't planned for or whatever thing that could come up that you need to pay immediately. Most families have to go into debt to pay for those kinds of unexpected expenditures which means they incur related interest costs and their budgets are strained because of the additional monthly payment until the debt is paid off.

But the smart way to operate is to set aside provision for those unexpected occasions. We recommend that the minimum a family should have set aside is $2,000 and that it should be deposited into some special savings account that's not so easy for you to get access to and take out funds for expenditures that aren't really emergencies. Just start setting aside an affordable portion of each pay check with the objective of building up to the $2,000 recommended MINIMUM. With this amount you'll be fairly well covered for most emergencies.

But don't stop there. You want to go on and continue slowly building your Contingency Fund until it reaches 6 times your monthly gross earnings. If your gross salary/income (before payroll deductions) is for example $3,000 per month then you'll want your eventual Contingency Fund to reach an ultimate objective of $18,000. Why? So you'll be covered for a period of time if you lose your job or your hours are cut back or if another recession comes along or you have a medical issue that makes it impossible for you to work for a few months. If you have your 6-month fund put together and you minimize your living expenses while you're going through the storm, it will be relatively for you and won't have to go into debt to make it through. You'll come out on the other side still Debt Free and still *financially successful*.

8. You Must Study to Become Informed

Finally, if you want to be *financially successful* it's absolutely essential that you study and become informed about the financial industry and how it operates. Most people don't know anything about it and yet our money is one of our most important interests in life. Your quality of life depends largely on how you handle your money yet most people don't know anything about it. They don't think they have to know, they don't want to invest the time it takes to learn about it and so they stay financially ignorant and live life mostly in chronic lack and insufficiency... There is a scripture in the Bible that really fits this situation: *"people are destroyed for a lack of knowledge."* If you attach the importance to your financial situation that it deserves you WILL study and make it a regular part of your life.

There're books and magazines you should be reading, there're FREE workshops and seminars you could be attending, there're many, many financial newsletters you can subscribe to. And of course the financial information available on the Internet is inexhaustible. The only question is this: is financial success important enough to you that you'll put in the time and attention that's needed to qualify for it? People who're financially uninformed will NEVER be *financially successful* because they'll make too many costly mistakes. You cannot short cut what it takes to be successful. No, you have to methodically and faithfully and repeatedly and continually do ALL the little things that it takes to get to where you want to be. Frankly, handling money correctly should be one of your highest priorities in life even ahead of your own job because if you work hard to be good in your job and make a good salary only to waste away the money you make after you bring it home, what good did it do? You had in your hands the means to become *financially successful* but wasted the opportunity by failing to give it a high enough priority. So go study now and learn everything you can find on the subject of your finances. You'll NEVER regret it.

Conclusions

As we wrap up this discussion, there're a few final key thoughts for you to always remember about becoming *financially successful:*

1) These eight basic secrets WILL produce financial success. It's guaranteed!
2) No matter the income level every person can be successful.
3) The only limits on your financial accomplishments are put there by you.
4) There're no short cuts to success.
5) You cannot circumvent the basic secrets we've discussed in this article.

If we can help you in any way please feel free to contact our ministry and when you call mention this article. Many of our services are FREE and our mission is to teach people what they need to know to be *financially successful*. Just call us at 305-271-5094 or toll free 1-800-357-4223. May God fully bless you and your family as you apply yourselves to the task of becoming *financial successful*.

ABOUT THE AUTHOR

Dr. Bill Miller is an ordained cross-denominational minister, elder and the founder of a national nonprofit Christian organization called *Make A Way Ministries.* He has been involved in financial counseling and teaching since 1985 and has assisted tens of thousands of families to overcome financial problems and get on to financial success and victory.

He also pastored the bilingual (English/Spanish) *Faith Life Fellowship Church* in Miami Florida from 2007 until 2012.

Dr. Miller has published a bible-based financial e-newsletter called *Prosperous Life Newsletter* since January 1998 and has written more than 25 books about various financial topics with the purpose of helping families overcome financial problems on a practical level.

Make A Way Ministries started officially in 1987 by counseling Christian business people in Dade County, Florida. That form of counseling has always been a particular calling for this ministry and provided a wealth of experience to draw from for this book.

Dr. Bill was born in Houston, Texas a long time ago and is a graduate of *Texas Tech University* in Lubbock. He also holds a Doctorate in Ministry from *Miami Christian University.*

He currently lives happily and works busily with his wife Sherri in the historic community of Granbury, Texas.

www.ingramcontent.com/pod-product-compliance
Lightning Source LLC
Chambersburg PA
CBHW071200240526
45470CB00017B/432